# Mental Subnormality

# Mental Subnormality

## Subnormality and Severe Subnormality

**by W. Alan Heaton-Ward,**
**MB, ChB, FRCPsych, DPM**
Consultant Psychiatrist
Stoke Park Hospital Group, Bristol
Clinical Teacher in Mental Health
University of Bristol

Fourth Edition

BRISTOL: JOHN WRIGHT & SONS LTD.
1975

First edition, May, 1960
Reprinted, September, 1961
Second edition, February, 1963
Reprinted, January, 1966
Third edition, August, 1967
Fourth edition, January, 1975

ISBN 0 7236 0376 6

Printed in Great Britain by John Wright & Sons Ltd.

*To the memory of*
*my friend and teacher*
*Dr John Francis Lyons*

# Preface to the Fourth Edition

SINCE the third edition was published in 1967, steady progress has continued in our understanding of the aetiology and possibilities of prevention of mental subnormality, so that we are now able to ascribe a definite cause to over 50 per cent of cases. The late Professor Lionel Penrose was able to revise his figures quoted in the previous edition and to ascribe a primarily genetic cause of mental subnormality in about 37 per cent of cases and a primarily environmental cause in about 20 per cent of cases.

In June, 1971, the Department of Health and Social Security and the Welsh Office published the Command White Paper 4683, *Better Services for the Mentally Handicapped*. According to the White Paper, there were in 1969, 58 850 patients resident in National Health Service hospitals or hospital units for the mentally handicapped (apart from those occupying beds in psychiatric hospitals for the mentally ill). The figures quoted in the White Paper indicate a steady increase in numbers between 1954 and 1968 when they reached 59 400 and that the reduction of 550 between 1968 and 1969 was in the age ranges 0–14 years and 15–54 years. However, there had been a steady increase in the number of patients aged 55 and over from 5500 in 1954 to 13 850 in 1969.

The White Paper suggests that the fall in the number of children 'may reflect the development of local authority services for children outside hospital'. However, the White Paper estimates a need for a further 4000 places for the residential care of children in the community and for a further 31 950 similar places for adults. *Mind Report No. 5*, published in December, 1971, following a survey carried out by the National Association for Mental Health, indicated a small improvement in local authority provisions for the residential care of the mentally handicapped since the surveys on which the figures in the White Paper were based were carried out. More recent reports of government refusal to grant loan sanction for many local authorities' plans for the mentally handicapped suggest that there is little prospect of their making adequate provision for their care in the community by the target dates in the White Paper and that the much criticized mental subnormality hospitals will have to continue for many years to provide the major part of the residential care for the mentally handicapped, who are unable to live with their families. *Mind Report No. 11,* published in October, 1973, shows that local authorities had been able to narrow the gap between the estimated need for 48 900 additional places for the occupation and training of mentally handicapped adults living in the community and the 1969 provision of 24 600 by only 2240.

# Acknowledgements

THE author is grateful to the many people who have sent him reprints of their own papers, which have been invaluable in preparing this new edition, and, as always, to Dr Jozé Jancar for his constant support and helpful discussions on many of the topics in this book. He is grateful, too, to Dr J. E. M. Glancy and Mr K. R. Pennington for their advice on consequential amendments to the Mental Health Act, 1959 as the result of subsequent legislation, and to Professor A. K. M. Macrae and Dr B. G. Scally for similar advice concerning the Mental Health Acts of 1960 and 1961 respectively. He wishes to thank, also, Mrs Joy Fearnley-Taylor for once again deciphering his handwriting and typing the manuscript, and Mr A. N. Boyd, Senior Editor of the publishers, for his advice.

*W. Alan Heaton-Ward*
*Clifton*
*Bristol 8*
*November, 1973*

# Contents

# The Concept of Mental Subnormality

THE Mental Health Act of 1959 recognizes two degrees of mental subnormality: 'severe subnormality' and 'subnormality', which it defines as follows.

SECTION 4 (2)—'severe subnormality' means a state of arrested or incomplete development of mind, which includes subnormality of intelligence, and is of such a nature or degree that the patient is incapable of living an independent life or of guarding himself against serious exploitation, or will be so incapable when of an age to do so.

SECTION 4 (3)—'subnormality' means a state of arrested or incomplete development of mind (not amounting to 'severe subnormality'), which includes subnormality of intelligence, and is of a nature or degree which requires or is susceptible to medical treatment or other special care or training of the patient.

While recognizing that 'mind' is something more than intelligence alone, embracing as it does other facets of an individual such as personality, character and temperament, the definition makes it clear that a person is not to be considered mentally subnormal merely because he shows defects of these other facets unless he is, in addition, subnormal in intelligence, although it makes no attempt to define what is meant by the latter.

In specifying a 'state of arrested or incomplete development of mind' the definition makes it clear that mental subnormality is to include both the cases where potentially normal mental development is arrested at some stage by environmental factors such as injury or disease and those cases where the potentiality for normal development has never been present from the time of conception owing to genetic defects.

It will be seen that the criterion of severe subnormality is ultimately a social one—namely, the incapacity for independent existence or for protecting oneself against serious exploitation, e.g. by an unscrupulous employer or in the sexual sphere. In the latter connection it is not generally realized that severely subnormal men are on occasions sexually exploited by women of higher intelligence just as, more frequently, severely subnormal women are exploited by men.

The severely subnormal category, therefore, includes all those patients who in the past were classified as idiots and imbeciles and a

1

large proportion of the feeble-minded class. On the other hand, the criterion of subnormality is less clearly defined. From the omission of the relevant part of the definition of severe subnormality it can be inferred that the concept of subnormality is not incompatible with the ability for independent existence, nor for guarding oneself against serious exploitation. However, the incapacity has to be of such a nature or degree as to require or to be susceptible to medical treatment or other special training of the patient. This category, therefore, would appear to include many on the indefinite borderline of normal intelligence, who constitute a large proportion of the social problem group, whose disabilities are manifest in general inefficiency and inadequacy rather than in the persistent abnormally aggressive or seriously irresponsible conduct which are the criteria in the Act (Section 4 (4)) of psychopathic disorder. It will be seen, therefore, that the subnormal category includes some patients previously called 'feeble-minded' as well as many border-line cases not previously classifiable as mentally defective at all, but as dull and backward.

It will also be seen that, whereas the criterion of severe subnormality is that of social incapacity, the criterion in the case of subnormality is a clinical one, namely that the condition requires or is susceptible to medical treatment or other special care or training of the patient.

Although the definitions of subnormality and severe subnormality have in common the presence of subnormality of intelligence, they wisely do not distinguish between them in terms of IQ. There is, in fact, a wide range of IQ in patients who satisfy the criterion of severe subnormality at the time of their admission to hospital. As a result of treatment and training they may become capable of leading an independent life and guarding themselves against serious exploitation, and can then be properly reclassified as subnormal. For these reasons, any attempt to limit the classification of severe subnormality to persons with an IQ below 50 is both undesirable and not necessarily legally accurate.

Throughout this book the term 'mental subnormality' is used to refer to the 'subnormal' and 'severely subnormal' groups collectively, and the latter terms are used whenever it is desired to refer to one or other group specifically. There is an understandable tendency to use 'subnormal' and 'subnormality' as collective terms, but this is apt to lead to confusion and, in view of the very different legal and prognostic implications of the two subgroups, is best avoided.

2

# The Developing Child

THE normal state for the newborn child is complete dependence on its mother for all its wants: food, warmth, security, affection and hygiene. However, from the moment of birth the baby normally becomes increasingly aware of its surroundings and independent of its mother. The more important of the stages by which independence is reached are known as the 'milestones' of development. All children do not develop at the same rate, but it is possible to quote an average age for the attainment of each milestone. As a general rule, boys tend to lag behind girls in all aspects of development.

A newly born baby shows a number of primitive reflexes, e.g. the 'placing' reflex, in which the foot is bent upwards and raised when the front of the leg is placed against the edge of a hard object; the 'walking' reflex, in which the legs are flexed and then extended when the baby is held with the soles of its feet on something solid; the 'grasp' reflex, in which the fingers or toes close into a grip when the palm or sole is stroked; the 'Moro' reflex, in which the baby shoots out its arms and opens its hands as if trying to save itself from falling, and then closes its arms together, when support is suddenly removed from behind its head; the 'rooting' reflex, in which the baby searches with its mouth for the nipple when its cheek comes in contact with its mother's breast. The walking reflex is normally lost by the end of the first month and the other reflexes by about the fourth month, as myelinization of the central nervous system proceeds. Other important reflexes concern the bowels and bladder, which empty automatically without respect for time, place or person.

By about the age of 4 months the average baby can hold its head off the pillow, and by between the fifth and seventh month its eye movements are co-ordinated so that it can follow an object without squinting. By about the seventh month it can sit unaided, by about 12 months it can stand and by about 18 months it can walk.

By the end of 12 months the average child can pick up small objects between the tips of the first finger and thumb. Its manual co-ordination improves, so that by the age of 18 months it can carry food successfully to its mouth with a spoon. By this age, too, the child is beginning to prefer to use one hand to the other. It normally has control of its bowels, and by the age of 2 years of its bladder

3

also, although this latter control may be disturbed, particularly at night, until a much later age owing to emotional stresses.

Other motor skills gradually develop, so that at 3 years the average child can feed itself with a spoon and fork and can copy drawings of simple shapes, but not draw them from memory. By the age of 5 years the average child can wash, dress and undress itself, and can use a knife, fork and spoon skilfully.

One of the most important milestones is the development of language. Understanding of spoken words precedes a child's own use of words. Thus at 12 months a child is learning to obey commands and to understand the meaning of 'no'. Its own vocabulary is restricted to one or two meaningful words. The understanding of words and phrases increases rapidly between 1 and 2 years. The use of words advances less rapidly, the difference being more marked in boys than girls. However, by the age of 2 years the average child has a vocabulary of several hundred words, which it can use to form short sentences to express its wants and feelings, and by the age of 5 years its vocabulary has grown to 2000 words. With increased vocabulary and understanding develops, ultimately, the ability to form abstract concepts such as morality and loyalty, understanding of which is essential before the child can take its full place in society.

**Piaget's Concepts**

Piaget claims that a child's intellectual development proceeds in the following stages, in which different kinds of thinking always succeed one another in the same order:

1. *Sensory-motor Stage*

During this stage the child is concerned only with objects it can directly perceive and it gains experience of them by handling and manipulating them. This stage normally ends at the age of about 18 months and is followed by the pre-conceptual stage.

2. *Pre-conceptual Stage*

During this stage the child is developing its ability to respond to objects in their absence, i.e. that it cannot directly perceive, as, for example, when it searches for a lost toy. It is developing its memory images, its powers of imaginative play and of language.

3. *Intuitive Thinking Stage*

During this stage, which normally begins at the age of about 4 years, the child's thinking is once again dominated by what it actually sees in front of it, and it makes no attempt to relate it to previous events. As a result it cannot, for example, understand that the total quantity of a fluid has remained the same when it has seen it poured from a glass container of one shape into another of obviously different shape and size. This stage normally lasts until the age of 7 years and is followed by the concrete operational thinking stage.

### 4. Concrete Operational Thinking Stage

During this stage the child begins to relate events to those that have preceded them and to those that follow and can, therefore, understand numbers as a series. It is able also to take account of two factors at once and of other viewpoints apart from its own.

### 5. Abstract Operational Stage

During this final stage of intellectual development, which normally begins at the age of about 11 years, the child begins to reason on the conceptual level.

There is some disagreement amongst psychologists as to the validity of Piaget's concept of stages of intellectual development, but it is being found useful in assessing the abilities of mentally subnormal children and in planning more helpful and realistic teaching and training programmes for them.

In the early months of life the child's emotional life is centred entirely around its mother, who satisfies all its needs. At this stage the child is unaware of any separate existence, but has started to become aware of its existence as a separate individual by the time it is 2 years old. This awareness is normally complete by the age of 3 years. Although at this age the child is becoming more and more aware of reality, fantasy still plays a considerable part in its life for the next 2 years. At this stage, too, irrational fears and night terrors are at their peak.

The child's immediate horizon widens to include, first, the father and other members of the family, and then individuals and groups outside its own family. The speed and extent to which this occurs depend on the parents' handling of this stage. At first, the child sees other children as rivals for its mother's affection and tends to revert to more infantile levels of behaviour in search of reassurance from its mother. The wise parent, while providing a consistent background of encouragement and security and affection, will not overprotect the child from environmental stresses, but will teach it to face them and adapt itself to them if they cannot be overcome. In this way the child's emotional development keeps pace with its intellectual development. However, parental mishandling at this stage, whether in the direction of over-protection or a too sudden severing of parental and emotional ties, may distort emotional development and result in immaturity of personality and neurotic traits in later life, including the inability to form satisfactory emotional relationships with members of the opposite sex.

By the time the normal child is 15 years old the basic potentiality for independent existence is established, although the personality is at this stage still immature and continues to develop at varying rates and to varying degrees of maturity. From the interaction of intelligence, personality and environment evolves character—an individual's apparent ability to control and direct all his activities and desires.

In the case of the subnormal there is delay in reaching, and, in the case of the severely subnormal, failure to reach, these various stages of development and integration, as a result of which the majority of the latter class are permanently incapable of leading an independent existence, in spite of treatment and training.

# The Diagnosis of
# Mental Subnormality

THE diagnosis of mental subnormality, although ultimately a psychiatric responsibility, is one to which parents, general practitioners, paediatricians, school teachers, nurses and school medical officers, occupational therapists, psychologists and social workers all contribute. Recent years have seen the establishment of assessment clinics, often as joint enterprises of Regional Hospital Boards and Local Health Authorities, to which suspected cases of mental subnormality may be referred for diagnosis and advice concerning treatment and training. Where there is any doubt the patient is admitted temporarily to hospital for fuller investigation. There is no doubt that these clinics are much appreciated by parents and others responsible for the care of the mentally subnormal, but a disappointing feature has been the apparent reluctance of general practitioners themselves to refer patients directly as they would do to the out-patient clinics of other specialities.

The diagnosis of mental subnormality is rarely possible and, with few exceptions, unwise in the first 6 months of life. The most important exception is Down's syndrome. When the suspicions aroused at birth by the characteristic facial appearance and other physical features of this condition are confirmed by chromosome analysis, the ultimate presence of some degree of severe subnormality can be forecast with certainty. However, it is unwise at this stage to make a more precise estimate of the probable degree of mental subnormality as this can vary greatly within the severely subnormal range. The time and manner in which the parents' attention is drawn to their child's abnormality must be most carefully chosen, with due regard to the personality, stability and intelligence of them both. It is important that this should be done by someone with sufficient knowledge to give authoritative yet gentle answers to the inevitable questions which follow, and that the informing of the parents should not be delayed too long, lest they are previously brought face to face with the problem by ill-informed and callous acquaintances.

Mental subnormality manifests itself in the developing child as retardation in attaining the various stages of development towards independence previously described, e.g. by a failure at 6 months of age to respond to its mother's smiles and caresses or to look about and show interest in its surroundings or to make any attempt to sit up or to grasp objects with its hands as a normal child would do. Between the ages of 2 and 3 years the child is developing rapidly and it is during this period that the developmental delays in the mentally subnormal may first become obvious. The presence of mental subnormality can be suspected if the milestones are consistently delayed by a third or more of the age at which they are normally present, e.g. if the child cannot walk by the age of 2 years or say a short sentence by the age of about 3 years, provided purely physical causes have been excluded in each case. It cannot be stressed too strongly, however, that these are merely grounds for suspecting the presence of mental subnormality. The confirmation of the presence of this condition is a skilled task involving a complete assessment of all aspects of development, both physical and mental, with due allowance for adverse environmental influences. However, the author believes that, where parents press for definite diagnosis and prognosis, controlled pessimism is less harmful in the long run than unreasoned optimism, with its inevitable disappointments.

Severe subnormality, not previously detected, quickly manifests itself when schooling begins as an obvious inability to keep pace with other children, and the child's sense of frustration in this respect may be expressed in behaviour disorders which were not previously present. Inquiry will usually reveal the same delayed development in preschool days described above.

In the least severe degrees of mental subnormality the academic disturbance is much less obvious and the child may complete its schooling and go into the outside world before definite evidence of mental subnormality occurs in the form of social inefficiency and irresponsibility—there is inability to keep any job for longer than a few weeks or jobs are frequently changed for trivial and inadequate reasons; late hours are kept, often in undesirable company, and parental guidance ignored. It is in individuals of this type that the most complete assessment of the previous history and of the present condition, both mental and physical, is required before a definite diagnosis of mental subnormality is made.

Some cases of mental subnormality do not come to light until the individual is brought before the court on some, very often, relatively minor charge, or it may not become apparent until he is actually in prison, although this is uncommon nowadays with psychological examination of offenders a more general practice.

Once a diagnosis of mental subnormality is made in a family, advice is often sought by the parents concerning the probability of the condition occurring in later children. In the past much of this advice has been ill-founded, and it is highly desirable that it should in future be given only after the most careful consideration of all the relevant aspects, if possible by a specialist in human genetics who is best equipped to give statistically accurate forecasts of the probabilities.

Parents should be helped to be honest, first with themselves and later with other people, about the true nature of their child's disability. Unfortunately they are still sometimes encouraged by well-meaning, but misguided, persons to adopt all sorts of euphemisms to hide the true condition. The acceptance of the knowledge that one's own child is mentally subnormal is never easy and creates inevitable and understandable emotional stresses, but until parents can themselves learn to be honest about their children in this way it cannot reasonably be expected that the general public will learn to accept them without fear and prejudice.

The assessment of mental subnormality should not be a once and for all exercise as it has, unfortunately, been so often in the past, but should be an ongoing process with periodic review by members of the multidisciplinary team which made the original diagnosis.

# The Causes of
# Mental Subnormality

THE condition underlying the various degrees of mental subnormality is known as 'amentia'. Some cases of amentia are known to be due to a genetic abnormality in the child itself, determined at the moment of conception or during the subsequent stages of division of the fertilized ovum. Other cases, without a genetic abnormality, are due to environmental factors which interfere with the development of the brain during pregnancy, during birth or at any other stage in the child's life before the genetically determined limits of its intelligence have been reached, usually about the age of 15 or 16 years. Some cases of amentia arise from a combination of both genetic and environmental factors, as, for example, in 'subcultural' amentia. It must be stressed, however, that even with the most careful exploration of family histories of the mentally subnormal and most careful examination of the individual's own history, it is often not possible in our present state of knowledge to decide with certainty the causation of all cases. This is, in part, a reflection on the inaccuracy of our present microscopical and biochemical techniques, and it seems highly probable that improved and new techniques will elucidate the causation of many of these at present unclassified cases of amentia in due course.

## THE GENETIC BASIS OF INHERITANCE

The innumerable factors, known as 'genes', which determine the potential limits of the physical and mental characteristics of each individual, are carried in the fertilized female sex cell (ovum) by twenty-three pairs of bodies, known as 'chromosomes', half of which are derived from the male and half from the female parent. Twenty-two of the pairs are called 'autosomal' and the other pair 'sex' chromosomes—either two X chromosomes in females or one X and one Y chromosome in males.

Chromosomes may be cultured from white blood cells and skin fibroblasts. Staining the cultured chromosomes with Giesma dye, quinacrine mustard or acridine orange reveals fluorescent banding patterns which are specific for different chromosomes and provide a

10

positive means of identifying them. It is then possible to arrange chromosomes in pairs, each with a similar banding pattern, and to number the autosomal chromosome pairs from 1 to 22, in decreasing order of size, plus a pair of sex chromosomes, making a normal total chromosome count of 46.

In an alternative method of classification, chromosome pairs are identified as follows: pairs 1 to 3—Group A; pairs 4 and 5—Group B; pairs 6 to 12—Group C; pairs 13 to 15—Group D; pairs 16 to 18—Group E; pairs 19 and 20—Group F; and pairs 21 and 22—Group G, plus one pair of sex chromosomes.

Whereas individual chromosomes can be seen under the microscope, the presence or absence of a particular gene can only be inferred from the effects produced.

The genes for some characteristics are capable of over-riding the effects of the corresponding genes derived from the other parent—such genes are said to be 'dominant' with respect to the other genes, which are called 'recessive'. A recessive gene can express itself only when another recessive gene for the same characteristic is inherited from the other parent. However, since both parents normally carry at least one pair of genes for each characteristic, but contribute only one gene of each pair to the fertilized ovum, it will be seen from the diagram below that the chance of both recessive genes coming together is only 1 in 4 and that in the other 3 cases the effects of the dominant gene will be produced.

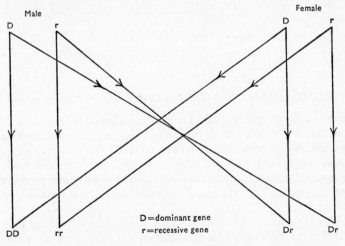

D=dominant gene
r=recessive gene

The genes which cause some cases of mental subnormality are carried on the sex chromosomes and are referred to as 'sex-linked'. The following diagram indicates how a sex-linked abnormality may be transmitted to male offspring by female carriers who themselves

11

escape, as do their female children. This is because the responsible gene, which is carried on one of the X chromosomes, is recessive to the corresponding normal gene on the other X chromosome of the female chromosome pair, but is able to act unopposed in the male, in whom the second X chromosome is absent. However, in the rare event of an affected male marrying a female carrier there is a theoretical risk of half of any female as well as male offspring being affected.

This very brief account of some of the principles of human genetics is included merely as an introduction to a most complex subject and in order to explain terms used later in this book.

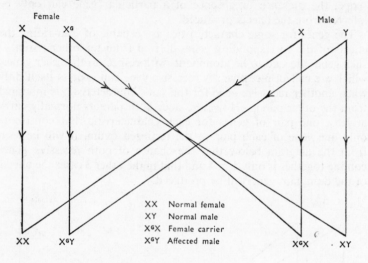

| | |
|---|---|
| XX | Normal female |
| XY | Normal male |
| X$^G$X | Female carrier |
| X$^G$Y | Affected male |

## CHROMOSOMAL ABNORMALITIES

Since 1959, a number of chromsomal abnormalities have been consistently demonstrated in various syndromes associated with amentia. These abnormalities have included the presence of extra whole autosomal and sex chromosomes, and the 'deletion' or absence of parts of chromosomes, resulting in an excess or diminution, respectively, of the genes normally carried on those chromosomes.

The presence of an extra chromosome with a banding pattern identical to that of a chromosome pair is known as a 'trisomy'. This arises from the failure of members of that particular pair of chromosomes to separate (non-disjunction) during the early stages of division of the mother's sex cells (meiosis) and results in a chromosome count of 47 after fertilization, instead of the normal 46.

Sometimes, usually during meiosis, one member from each of two different autosomal pairs may become attached together to produce a compound chromosome. This process is known as 'translocation' and results in an apparent total chromosome count of 45 instead of the normal 46, but as there is almost no diminution in the total normal gene complement, no physical or intellectual abnormality results. However, as will be seen later, translocations may in some cases be transmitted to offspring and result in both physical and intellectual abnormalities.

The absence of a whole autosomal chromosome from any pair appears to be a lethal condition, but the absence of one of the sex chromosomes is not incompatible with life, although it is associated with physical abnormalities and, in some cases, with impaired intelligence. It has been claimed that the physical effects of an excess of genes are exactly the opposite of those of a diminution of the same genes—the 'mirror-image theory'.

Less consistently reported chromosomal abnormalities in other syndromes in amentia include 'constrictions' in the body of the chromosomes, 'ring forms', in which the ends of a partially deleted chromosome become joined together, the presence of 'satellites' or small fragments attached to chromosomes, and 'interstitial translocations' in which part of one chromosome becomes incorporated in the corresponding part of another.

As a result of abnormal separation of chromosomes during the later stages of cell division (mitosis), chromosome 'mosaics' may occur in which a number of cells of the body contain an excess of chromosomes and the remainder a corresponding deficit.

## AMNIOCENTESIS

It is now possible to detect most autosomal and sex chromosome abnormalities during pregnancy by culturing chromosomes from a small quantity of amniotic fluid drawn off from the uterus at about the 14th week of pregnancy. This enables the mother to be offered the opportunity of termination of pregnancy where abnormalities are revealed.

Errors in diagnosis due to twin pregnancy may be avoided by the use of ultrasound, which enables the outline of each fetus to be defined with accuracy and less possible risk to the fetus than with radiography.

## DERMATOGLYPHICS

The increasing knowledge of significant chromosomal abnormalities has led to a renewed interest in finger-print and palm-print patterns, known as dermatoglyphics, and to an attempt to correlate specific patterns with specific chromosomal abnormalities. There are three basic finger-tip patterns, the 'whorl', the 'arch' and the 'loop'. Loops are referred to as 'radial' or 'ulnar' according to the direction in which they open. The density of the ridge systems, which make up these patterns, can be expressed numerically as the total ridge count for all ten fingers.

The palmar pattern is similarly made up of a number of ridge systems. The point where three ridge systems meet is known as a 'triradius'.

Particular attention is paid in dermatoglyphics to the relative incidence of the different types of finger-tip patterns, to the total ridge count and to the angle ('atd' angle) formed between the triradius at the base of the index finger (a), the most distal axial triradius on the palm of the hand (t), and the triradius at the base of the little finger (d). The normal 'atd' angle is about 48°.

## CASES OF AMENTIA WITH KNOWN GENETIC ABNORMALITIES

### A. AFFECTING CHROMOSOMES

The presence of extra, large chromosomes appears to be incompatible with life and may be found in fetuses which abort spontaneously. It is not until the thirteenth to fifteenth chromosomal pairs are reached that a fetus with an extra chromosome ('trisomy') becomes viable, but even then it has gross physical abnormalities and short expectation of life.

### AUTOSOMAL TRISOMIES

#### 1. Trisomy 13–15, Group D Trisomy (Patau's Syndrome)

The incidence of this trisomy is about 0·1 per 1000 live births and is related to advancing maternal age. The risk of recurrence is low unless either parent is a translocation carrier. The most commonly reported features are a small head and receding chin, various eye defects, low-set deformed ears, hare-lip and cleft palate and polydactyly (extra fingers and toes). There are specific abnormalities in the brain and congenital heart abnormalities may be present. Dermatoglyphics show an increase in the frequency of radial loops in the finger-tip patterns and there is often a single transverse palmar crease ('simian crease'). The 't' triradius is very distally placed, resulting in a very wide 'atd' angle of over 100°. A proximally placed tibial loop is commonly found on the hallucal area of the sole of the foot.

14

The degree of mental subnormality is severe and it is rare for infants with Patau's syndrome to live for more than 6 months.

### 2. Trisomy 17–18, Group E Trisomy (Edwards's Syndrome)

The incidence of this trisomy is about 0·5 per 1000 live births and is related to advancing maternal age. It occurs about twice as frequently in females as in males. The risk of recurrence is small unless either parent is a translocation carrier. The features of trisomy 17–18 overlap to a considerable degree those of trisomy 13–15. However, the most commonly reported features of trisomy 17–18 are anteroposterior elongation of the skull, receding chin, low-set deformed ears, webbing of the neck, congenital heart defects, fingers which are flexed and tend to overlap, retroflexible and distally placed thumbs, limited hip abduction, 'rocker bottom' feet, short, dorsiflexed big toes and spasticity. The toenails are often hypoplastic. In the brain the frontal lobes of the cerebral hemispheres fail to separate normally.

Dermatoglyphics show a striking preponderance of arches in the finger-tip patterns, forming over 80 per cent of all patterns in infants with this syndrome. The 't' triradius may be distally displaced, but less so than in trisomy 13–15. As in Patau's syndrome, the degree of mental subnormality in Edwards's syndrome is severe and affected infants have a poor sucking reflex and rarely live for more than 6 months. However, a case of apparent trisomy 18 has been reported in a girl of nearly 9 years who was severely subnormal, with a small, round head, low hairline on the neck, shallow orbits, deformed ears, beaked nose, small mouth, high arched palate and underdeveloped teeth, scoliosis, shield-like chest with underdeveloped nipples, heart murmur, small external genitalia, flexion contractures of the arms and fingers with ulnar deviation and bilateral simian creases, and flexion contractures of the legs with bilateral club feet.

Dermatoglyphics showed hypoplastic dermal ridges, with arches on all the finger tips of both hands.

### 3. Trisomy 21, Group G Trisomy (Down's Syndrome; Mongolism)

Trisomy 21 is, in fact, a misnomer. When the presence of an extra small acrocentric chromosome was discovered in Down's syndrome in 1959 it was thought to be identical to members of pair 21. However, the fluorescent banding patterns of the extra chromosome are those of pair 22. Down's syndrome should, therefore, be correctly called trisomy 22, but to avoid confusion, it has been decided by international agreement to continue to refer to Down's syndrome as trisomy 21.

In about 4–5 per cent of cases of Down's syndrome, the extra chromosome has become attached to a member of another pair of chromosomes to produce a 13/21, 15/21, 21/21 or 21/22 translocation. The resulting compound chromosome has the appearance of a single chromosome, so that the total chromosome count appears to be 46 instead of the 47 expected in any trisomic condition. Either parent may be the carrier of such a translocation and will have an apparent total chromosome count of only 45. In some cases of Down's syndrome the total chromosome count is higher than 47 due to the presence of one or more extra female X chromosomes, which are accompanied by various abnormalities of sexual development.

The overall incidence of Down's syndrome is 1·8 per 1000 (1 in 600) live births, but the incidence ranges from about 1 in 2000 live births at the lower end of the child-bearing period to about 1 in 50 live births at the end of that period. Down's syndrome occurs in most races and cases have been reported in Chinese, Japanese and Negroes. Parents frequently avoid having any more children after the birth of a child with Down's syndrome, so that the child's most common position in the family is either first (and only) or last, but up to 5 cases among siblings have been reported, as well as identical twins with Down's syndrome and twins in which one had Down's syndrome and the other was quite normal.

The cause of the non-disjunction resulting in the trisomic condition in Down's syndrome (whether translocated or not) cannot, as yet, be stated categorically, but a number of relevant facts are known.

Cases of Down's syndrome may be divided into two groups: one in which the incidence is independent of the maternal age at the time of conception and the other in which it is dependent on that factor. The first group is numerically smaller than the second and contains both trisomic and translocation cases, the latter being in the minority. In some of these cases the translocation is transmitted by a parent and in others arises sporadically. A proportion of cases are born to mothers who are, in fact, themselves Down's syndrome mosaics.

As already stated, the incidence of Down's syndrome increases with advancing maternal age at the time of conception, but the reason for this is not yet known. Virus infection (particularly infectious hepatitis) in the mother, or immunization of the mother with live viruses, maternal exposure to radiation, either diagnostic or random, increased maternal thyroid antibodies, lowered urinary oestriol excretion during pregnancy and altered pH of the blood, have all been suggested as possibly significant aetiological factors in Down's syndrome. However, none has, as yet, received general

16

acceptance, but it is possible that the chromosomal abnormalities in Down's syndrome may be brought about by a wide variety of different factors, including those just mentioned.

## Clinical Features

Babies with Down's syndrome are often born before their expected date of delivery with a low birth weight. The typical features of Down's syndrome are present at birth. Facially they bear a strong resemblance to each other. The skull is brachycephalic due to the failure of its basal segments to elongate normally. As a result, the head in Down's syndrome is small and round, the transverse and anteroposterior diameters are almost the same and the back of the skull is flattened. The hair on the scalp does not, in the author's experience, differ as much in texture from the normal as is often suggested. However, the beard and axillary hair are scanty and the pubic hair is straight. The palpebral fissures slope downwards and inwards and often the upper eyelid overlaps the lower at the inner canthus, the so-called 'epicanthic fold'. Various abnormalities in the eyes themselves occur. Very frequently there is a fine white speckling of the iris known as 'Brushfield spots'. Cataracts may be present, as may be strabismus or nystagmus. The nose is small, with a poorly developed bridge which makes the eyes look farther apart than normal, whereas the opposite is, in fact, the case. The ears are small, of simple pattern, and often with poorly developed lobes. The palate is high, arched and short and the tongue tends to protrude, although it is not usually much larger than normal. It shows various degrees of transverse furrowing. The teeth develop late and may be abnormal in their size, shape and alignment.

The neck is short and thick, so that sometimes the head appears to be set directly on the shoulders. The limbs are shorter than normal and, even when fully grown, people with Down's syndrome are well below normal height. The pelvis shows constant variations from the normal, which produce a diagnostic appearance on X-ray examination. The muscles generally are hypotonic, enabling joints to be hyper-extended and strange postures to be adopted. The abdomen is protuberant and an umbilical hernia may be present.

Next to the facial appearance the hands are the most typical feature of Down's syndrome: the palm is square and a transverse palmar crease ('four-finger line' or simian crease) occurs in between 30 and 40 per cent of cases; the fingers, which may be webbed (syndactyly), are shorter than normal, particularly the fifth finger, which may not extend beyond the first interphalangeal joint of the fourth finger. In over 50 per cent of cases it may be incurving (clinodactyly), with only a single flexion crease in about 25 per cent of cases. The thumb, too, is shorter than normal and may extend only to the metacarpophalangeal joint of the index finger.

The great toe, also, is shorter than normal and is separated from the second toe by a wide gap which may extend as a cleft onto the sole of the foot. Syndactyly of the toes may be present. The dermatoglyphic patterns of the hands and feet in Down's syndrome are pathognomonic and may enable a diagnosis to be made in doubtful cases before a chromosome analysis can be completed. In Down's syndrome the most distal triradius is near the centre of the palm, so that the 'atd' angle (about 80°) is almost twice the normal. The finger-tip patterns show fewer whorls and arches than in the general population. The number of radial loops is reduced and the number of ulnar loops increased, occurring on all 10 fingers in over 30 per cent of cases of Down's syndrome. Where radial loops are present in Down's syndrome they are typically on one or both ring fingers. The typical palm print shows a large hypothenar pattern, a very small or absent thenar pattern and a digital loop between the bases of the third and fourth fingers. Another typical feature is the absence of any pattern on the hallucal area of the sole in about 50 per cent of cases of Down's syndrome.

Congenital cardiac abnormalities are far less commonly present in adults with Down's syndrome than is usually believed, possibly because they have caused death at an early age—slightly over 50 per cent of all children with Down's syndrome die during the first year of life. However, peripheral circulatory disturbances are common and in cold weather the lips, hands and feet are often cyanosed and chilblains occur. Congenital abnormalities of other internal organs may also be present such as atresia of the upper part of the gastrointestinal tract. Hirschsprung's disease (congenital dilatation of the colon) frequently occurs in Down's syndrome. The brain in Down's syndrome is smaller than normal with simplification of the gyral pattern.

People with Down's syndrome are characteristically mouth breathers and are very prone to severe respiratory infections, which previously caused their early death, but with the introduction of antibiotics their expectation of life has increased considerably. At the beginning of the century it was rare for anyone with Down's syndrome to survive in hospital beyond his tenth birthday. Now the average age of death of such a patient is approaching 30 years. Patients with Down's syndrome cared for in hospitals appear to be more susceptible to infections than other groups, although the increased susceptibility seems to be greater in males than females. However, both sexes are very prone to chronic blepharitis, due to the absence from the tears of the enzyme lysozyme, which normally

18

prevents infection. There is evidence that patients with Down's syndrome in hospital may provide a reservoir for human viral hepatitis and infect other patients without ever showing clinical signs of jaundice themselves. Lymphocytic thyroiditis occurs in about 30 per cent of cases of Down's syndrome, affecting females more frequently than males.

Epilepsy and cerebral palsy are rare accompaniments of Down's syndrome, possibly because the brachycephalic skull undergoes relatively little moulding during labour, with consequently reduced risk of brain damage due to abnormal compression.

It has been believed for some years that children with Down's syndrome run twenty times the random risk of developing acute leukaemia, but it has recently been suggested that transient leukaemoid reactions which are rare in normal children may, in the past, have been mistaken for true leukaemia in children with Down's syndrome and that the incidence of true leukaemia may be the same in both types of children.

The mean red cell volume has been shown to be abnormally increased in many non-anaemic patients with Down's syndrome, but the significance of this finding is not at present understood. A large number of studies of erythrocyte enzymes in Down's syndrome have been carried out with conflicting results.

People with Down's syndrome vary widely in their degree of mental incapacity within a wide range of IQ and achievements, including, in some cases, the ability to read and write, but all chromosomally confirmed cases fall within the severely subnormal category judged on the criterion of their inability to lead an independent existence. Their practical ability exceeds their reasoning ability. Most sit by the age of 1 year and learn to walk between the ages of 2 and 3 years. They have an outstanding capacity for mimicry (in which they are no respecters of persons!) and it is this which makes them appear brighter intellectually than in fact they are. They are affectionate and characteristically cheerful, and, although often mischievous, as a group are the most easily managed of all ambulant mentally subnormal patients. They are musical and have a strongly developed sense of rhythm. In spite of their superficial similarity as regards physical appearance and temperamental characteristics, they show many personal variations and should therefore always be treated as individuals.

The libido is very much reduced in Down's syndrome. There is no record of a male with Down's syndrome fathering a child and there are only 13 published cases of females with Down's syndrome giving birth. In only 5 cases did the child itself suffer from the same condition. Evidence suggests that it is only the translocation type of Down's syndrome which is transmissible to the child.

19

Some mentally subnormal people show only partial features of Down's syndrome and are usually of more normal stature and higher intelligence. Such people are best described as 'mongoloid'. They frequently show the mosaic pattern on chromosome analysis, with the extra 21 chromosomes present in only half the body's cells and with dermatoglyphic patterns intermediate between those of true trisomy 21 and the normal.

## Genetic Counselling

The risk to parents who have already had a child with regular trisomy 21 of having another child similarly affected is about 1 in 100, irrespective of the age of the mother. However, the risk is greatly increased if either parent is the carrier of a translocated 21 chromosome, e.g. in the case of 15/21 translocation the risk is about 1 in 10 where the mother is the carrier, and about 1 in 20 where the father is the carrier. In the case of 21/22 translocation the risks are slightly higher, about 1 in 6 where the mother is the carrier, and about 1 in 12 where the father is the carrier. However, where either the mother or the father is the carrier of the fortunately rare 21/21 translocation, all their children will have Down's syndrome. Advancing paternal age at the time of conception appears to be a significant factor in the 21/22 translocation group.

It has recently been suggested that one-third to one-half the mothers with more than one child with Down's syndrome are themselves Down's mosaics. However, genetically transmitted forms of Down's syndrome appear, on present evidence, to account for less than 2 per cent of all cases so that the prevention of such cases would have little effect on the prevalence of this condition. On the other hand, the incidence of Down's syndrome could be reduced by a half by the detection by amniocentesis and subsequent termination of pregnancy in all positive cases in women aged 35 and over.

## OTHER AUTOSOMAL CHROMOSOMAL ABNORMALITIES

### Partial Trisomies

Mental subnormality may be associated with the presence of extra chromosome material which can be identified as similar to that of part of a chromosome in the normal chromosome complement.

### 1. *Chromosome 4–5 Group B*

The presence of extended long arms in one member of a pair in the 4–5 chromosome group B has not yet been shown to produce a constant and specific physical syndrome, but the following abnormalities have been associated with it: reduced stature and weight, microcephaly, anti-mongoloid slope of the eyes, epicanthic folds, moderate ptosis, hypertelorism, beak-shaped nose, high narrow palate, widely spaced incisors and malshaped ears and narrow ear canals.

Dermatoglyphics have been reported as showing a simian crease, wide 'atd' angles and reduced ridge counts.

### 2. *Mosaic Trisomy* 8

Physical abnormalities reported in this condition include strabismus, large ears, everted lower lip, broad fingers with dystrophic finger nails, metatarsus–varus deformity and deep plantar creases.

Dermatoglyphics show the unusual presence of both arches and whorls on the finger tips and a whorl on the fourth interdigital area of the palm. The total finger ridge count is low and a simian crease may be present. The pattern intensity on the soles is high with an increase in the number of whorls, including the very rare type on the fourth interdigital area.

### 3. *Partial Trisomy* 15

Children with partial trisomy 15 are less severely handicapped physically and mentally than those with full trisomy 13–15 (Patau's syndrome). They are below normal in stature and weight. Physical abnormalities described include antimongoloid shape of the eyes, alternating strabismus, epicanthic folds, wide nasal bridge, large mouth with full lips and widely spaced teeth, large ears, mild thoracic kyphosis, valgus deformity of the elbow, and spindle-shaped fingers, with a short fifth finger.

### Chromosome Deletions

### 1. *Chromosome 5—Deletion of Short Arm ('Cri du Chat' Syndrome)*

In this condition, which affects females more frequently than males, there is a partial deletion of the short arm of one of the fifth pair of chromosomes. Affected children usually have a low birth weight at maturity and subsequent growth is retarded. The facial appearance is not sufficiently specific to suggest the diagnosis—features most frequently reported are microcephaly, anti-mongoloid slope of the eyes, epicanthic folds, strabismus, a broad flattened nose with hypertelorism, low set ears and a small mouth. The main clue to the diagnosis is the characteristic cry of the newborn baby from which the syndrome derives its name; it is said to resemble the mewing cry of an injured kitten. This cry is believed to be associated with under-development of the upper part of the larynx. The degree of mental subnormality is severe.

As the child becomes older the typical cry disappears and other physical features appear, including dental malocclusion, short meta-carpals and metatarsals, small wings of the iliac bones of the pelvis, flat feet, prematurely greying hair and increasing spasticity and exaggerated reflexes.

Dermatoglyphics show a slight excess of whorls with a corre-sponding decrease in the number of ulnar loops in the finger-print patterns. A pattern on the fourth interdigital area is a frequent occurrence, as is the presence of a simian crease and the absence of thenar and hypothenar patterns.

The incidence of the 'cri du chat' syndrome is unrelated to maternal age, and the risk of recurrence is low unless either of the parents is the carrier of a translocation in which the deleted portion of the short arm of chromosome number 5 is attached to another chromosome.

### 2. *Chromosome 4—Deletion of Short Arm* (*Wolf's Syndrome*)

There is a partial deletion of the short arm of one chromosome in pair 4. A number of the features of this syndrome are similar to those of the 'cri du chat' syndrome, e.g. low birth weight and retarded growth, microcephaly, anti-mongoloid slope of the eyes, epicanthic folds, strabismus, a broad flattened nose with hypertelorism and a small mouth. However, the typical cry does not occur in Wolf's syndrome, in which other common distinguishing physical features are coloboma of the iris, preauricular and sacral dimples, cleft palate, fish-shaped mouth, hypospadias and delayed bone maturation. The degree of mental subnormality is more severe than that in the 'cri du chat' syndrome and seizures occur more frequently.

Dermatoglyphics show a lower ridge count than in the 'cri du chat' syndrome, with a higher frequency of arches on the finger tips, a higher frequency of double loops on the thumbs and a lower frequency of thenar and hypothenar patterns.

### 3. *Chromosome 18—Partial Deletion of Long Arm*

The deletion affects the long arm of one chromosome in pair 18. Children with this abnormality are small at birth and slow in their growth. They have small heads and a characteristic facial appearance. The middle part of the face is poorly developed, the eyes are deeply set and the bridge of the nose is underdeveloped. The chin, in con-trast, is well developed. There is a typical deformity of the external ears, with overdevelopment of the helix, antihelix and antitragus. The

22

muscular tone is generally poor. There is frequently a simian crease and the fingers and thumbs are usually long and tapering.

Dermatoglyphics show a high count of whorls on the fingers.

The degree of mental subnormality is moderate.

There is some evidence of immunoglobulin deficiency in this condition.

### 4. *Chromosome 21—Partial Deletion of Long Arm* ('*Antimongolism*')

When first described it was claimed that this syndrome illustrated well the 'mirror-image' theory already referred to and it was so called because the physical features were said to be the opposite of those in mongolism (Down's syndrome). However, it now appears that those most frequently described do not support this claim—they include cataract, broad nasal bridge, low-set ears, inguinal hernia, hypospadias, scrotal dysplasia and club foot.

### Ring Chromosomes

### 1. *Chromosome Group 6–12, Group C*

The presence of a ring chromosome in the chromosome group 6–12 has been reported in association with severe subnormality accompanied by various physical abnormalities of the face and limbs, but so far no constant picture has emerged.

### 2. *Chromosome Group 13–15, Group D* ('*Cat Eye*' *Syndrome*)

It seems probable that the ring in this syndrome arises from chromosome 13 from partial deletions of both its short and long arms. In some cases only the long arms are affected without the formation of a ring. The most commonly reported features are severe subnormality, microcephaly, coloboma of the iris, hypertelorism, malformed ears with preauricular skin tags or dimples, congenital heart disease, slender finger-like thumbs, clinodactyly of the fifth fingers, anal atresia, hypospadias, scrotal and perineal abnormalities in males and rectovaginal fistulae in females.

Dermatoglyphic reports have included the presence of ulnar loops on all the finger tips and radial arches in the hypothenar area, with absence of an axial triradius on both palms.

### SEX CHROMOSOMAL ABNORMALITIES

The presence of extra X chromosomes carries with it the increased risk of mental subnormality. In males, as a general rule, the greater the number of extra X chromosomes present the greater the physical deformity and the more severe the mental subnormality. This suggests that the inactivation of all but one X chromosome is only partial and not complete as the 'Lyonization' hypothesis requires. In females the effect is less marked. On the other hand, the absence of an X chromosome is not incompatible with normal intelligence. Thus, in Turner's syndrome with an XO complement, physical and sexual abnormalities occur, but mental subnormality is rare.

The partially inactivated X chromosomes in each cell become tightly coiled and, on staining, appear as dark masses (Barr bodies or sex chromatin masses) beneath the nuclear membrane. There is always one less Barr body present than the number of X chromosomes present in the cell—thus a normal female has one Barr body and is said to be 'chromatin positive' and the normal male no Barr body and is said to be 'chromatin negative'. There is an inverse ratio between the number of X chromosomes present and the total ridge count in the dermatoglyphics.

A number of mental subnormality syndromes are inherited in a sex-linked manner and when a pregnant woman is known to be a carrier of such a condition it is important for purposes of genetic counselling to determine the sex of the fetus. This may be done by staining cultured fetal fibroblast cells, obtained by amniocentesis, with quinacrine mustard, which produces distinctive fluorescent patterns by which Barr bodies and Y chromosomes can be distinguished with certainty in single pregnancies. However, in multiple pregnancies involving fetuses of different sexes, errors may occur unless cells are obtained from within each amniotic sac, located with the help of ultrasound. The abnormalities of the sex chromosomes associated with mental subnormality may be divided into three main sub groups:

## 1. Trisomy X (XXX Syndrome)

This syndrome has an overall incidence of nearly 1 in 1000 female births. It is estimated to occur in up to 1 per cent of mentally subnormal females. Like other sex chromosomal abnormalities its incidence is independent of maternal age. It produces no obvious physical or sexual abnormality and is, therefore, not always recognized. The degree of mental subnormality is slight. Affected women are usually fertile and give birth to normal children.

A number of cases with up to 2 extra X chromosomes have been reported, but cases with more than this are exceedingly rare and only 4 cases with 3 extra X chromosomes (Syndrome XXXXX) have so far been reported.

Women with the XXXXX syndrome are severely subnormal, with numerous skeletal abnormalities, many of which occur also in the XXXXY syndrome in males. Such abnormalities include deformities of the elbow, involving the ulna in particular, deformities of the wrist, again involving the ulna, clinodactyly of the fifth finger and deformities of the pelvis and knees which, as a result, tend to be held in a flexed position when standing. In females the breasts are poorly developed, the pubic hair is scanty and the uterus small.

Dermatoglyphics have shown the presence of arches on all 10 finger tips in 1 case.

## 2. Trisomy XY (XXY, Klinefelter's Syndrome)

This is the commonest sex chromosome abnormality and occurs in about 1 in 500 males, but in slightly over 1 per cent of all mentally subnormal males, most frequently in the less severely subnormal. Because of the presence of an extra X chromosome such cases have a Barr body and are referred to as chromatin positive. Children with this abnormality develop normally until puberty when the male secondary characteristics fail to appear, and in their place female bodily proportions and gynaecomastia may develop.

Affected individuals achieve performance IQ's on intelligence testing which are consistently higher than their verbal IQ's.

Klinefelter's syndrome may be associated with Down's syndrome so that the chromosome constitution is trisomy $21 + XXY$, giving a chromosome count of 48.

Less common, and progressively more severely subnormal, are those males who have up to three extra X chromosomes (XXXXY syndrome).

Affected males tend to be tall, due to delayed union of the epiphyses at the ends of the long bones, and they show many of the other skeletal abnormalities already discussed in the XXXXX syndrome. Their external genitalia and secondary sexual characteristics are under-developed.

As in XXXXX females dermatoglyphics show a low total ridge count and a preponderance of arches on the finger tips. The 'd' triradius has been found to be absent in some cases of the XXXXY syndrome.

## 3. XYY Syndrome

The latest surveys suggest that the incidence of this syndrome is about 1 in 700 males. It has also been reported in identical twins. Affected males are over 6 ft (183 cm) tall and are normal in their general physical and sexual development and do not transmit their chromosomal abnormality to their offspring. There is no consistent evidence of any hormonal abnormalities or of any connection between a variety of bone abnormalities which have been reported and the presence of the extra Y chromosome.

The first discovery of the XYY syndrome in the residents of the special hospitals for patients with criminal and antisocial tendencies understandably led to the suggestion of a causal relationship between the chromosomal abnormality and the behaviour disorder. However, it is now clear that there are a number of males with the XYY syndrome living in the community and showing none of these antisocial tendencies. The cases reported from special hospitals were mildly subnormal in intelligence, but there is so far no conclusive evidence that males with the XYY syndrome run a higher risk of having intelligence below the normal than unaffected males.

Recent surveys among patients with the XYY syndrome in special hospitals and forensic psychiatric clinics suggest that these patients have difficulties in making relationships and have few friends. They tend to be impulsive and hot-tempered and to be easily provoked into acts of violence because of their lack of self-control. However, their convictions have been more frequently for offences against property than against people and their criminal activities have often begun at a very young age. There is evidence that enlargement of the Y chromosome in males with an otherwise normal XY chromosome constitution may carry with it an increased risk of personality disorder and violent and criminal behaviour.

Some male patients have an extra X as well as an extra Y chromosome (XXYY syndrome). They show a similar tendency to violent behaviour but are characteristically more obviously mentally subnormal. Males with sex chromosome abnormalities in special hospitals have been reported as having a higher than expected prevalence of EEG abnormalities, which almost invariably involved the background activity with an increased frequency of slow wave activity.

### Sex Chromosome Mosaics

About one-third of all chromatin-positive males are XY/XXY mosaics and a third or more of all females with additional X chromosomes are mosaics.

### B. AFFECTING GENES

A number of syndromes associated with mental subnormality show no gross chromosomal abnormalities, but are due to abnormal genes.

Some of these syndromes can be recognized by the typical facial appearance. The most common is 'true' microcephaly.

## 1. 'TRUE' MICROCEPHALY

The skull is usually said to be microcephalic when its circumference is less than 17 in. in an adult. Environmental factors during pregnancy may interfere with the development of the brain and skull and result in microcephaly. These factors will be referred to later. In the case of 'true' microcephaly, however, the condition is inherited in an autosomal recessive manner with an incidence of about 1 in 1000 live births, and several children in the same generation of a family may be affected.

The striking feature of this condition is not merely the smallness of the head, but rather the marked disproportion between the face of a normal size and the tiny cranial vault. In profile the appearance is characteristic, with a markedly receding chin and forehead. Sometimes the scalp has a corrugated appearance ('cutis verticis gyrata'), but this condition is not confined to microcephaly and its aetiology is unknown. It occurs mostly in males, in whom it develops slowly between the ages of 20 and 30 years. These patients are usually short in stature and may have various associated neurological abnormalities. A number suffer from epilepsy.

The majority are within the severely subnormal range, although some may be subnormal. They are usually pleasant in manner and well behaved.

Apart from its overall small size, the brain may show various developmental abnormalities: there may be a failure of development of the secondary gyri or the gyri may be very much narrower than normal ('microgyria') or there may be large cystlike spaces in the substance of the brain ('porencephaly').

## 2. BIRD-HEADED DWARF (VIRCHOW-SECKEL-DWARF)

This condition is inherited in an autosomal recessive manner.

Affected children are small for their gestational age and are of slender body build. They have a bird-like appearance due to microcephaly, prominent eyes, hypoplasia of the malar bones, a prominent, sometimes beaked nose and a receding chin. The ears are lowset, with absent lobes. The palate is high and arched and may be cleft. The teeth may be absent or atrophic and the enamel hypoplastic.

There may be skeletal abnormalities such as dislocation of the head of the radius and congenital dislocation of the hips, with wide spacing between the first and second toes.

Mild to moderate mental subnormality occurs.

## 3. ACROCEPHALO-SYNDACTYLY (APERT'S SYNDROME)

This syndrome is inherited in an autosomal dominant manner, but the gene concerned has poor penetrance so that only partial features of the disease may occur.

The facial appearance is characteristic. The skull is oxycephalic, i.e. it is elongated upwards, hence the description 'tower skull' or 'steeple skull' sometimes applied. On X-ray examination the skull may be thinned and its inner table may show a 'copper-beaten' appearance. The eyes are markedly protuberant. The palate is high and narrow like a Gothic arch and the teeth are very irregular.

The facial appearance is due to the premature fusion of the bones in the base of the skull, so that the orbits are shallow and the brain, being unable to develop laterally, has to do so vertically, expanding the skull in the same direction.

There are gross abnormalities of the hands and feet. The fingers and toes may be entirely rudimentary or may be fused with adjacent fingers or toes.

The degree of mental subnormality varies.

## 4. CRANIOFACIAL DYSOSTOSIS (CROUZON'S SYNDROME)

This syndrome is inherited in a similar manner to that of acrocephalo-syndactyly and produces a somewhat similar facial appearance and similar X-ray appearances of the skull. However, in contrast to that condition, limb abnormalities do not occur and mental subnormality is present in only about 20 per cent of cases.

## 5. HYPERTELORISM (GREIG'S SYNDROME)

This condition appears to be inherited in an irregularly autosomal dominant manner in some families and in an autosomal recessive manner in others.

The condition is characterized by the typical facial appearance, in which the bridge of the nose is broad and flattened and the eyes are very widely set. This is due to overgrowth of that part of the sphenoid bone in the base of the skull which develops from cartilage. The palate is usually high and narrow, like a Gothic arch.

Hypertelorism, in which the distance between the eyes themselves is, in fact, greater than normal, has to be distinguished from 'telecanthus', in which the appearance is similar but in that case due to an increased distance between the inner canthi of the lids of the two eyes.

In some cases, the fingers and toes are similar to those in Down's syndrome and a connection has been suggested between the two conditions. Another feature common to both conditions is the incidence of congenital heart defects.

Mentally, those affected are usually within the severely subnormal range, although on occasions they are classifiable as subnormal and in rare cases are of normal intelligence.

Hypertelorism may also occur as a feature of other genetically determined syndromes associated with mental subnormality.

## 6. *FIRST ARCH SYNDROMES*

Mental subnormality of varying degree occurs in several of the syndromes associated with abnormal development of the structures arising embryologically from the first branchial arch. There is a considerable overlap of the features of the various syndromes in this group:

### a. **Cervico-oculo-acoustic Dysplasia (Syndrome of Wildervanck)**

The mode of inheritance of this syndrome is not known with certainty. The main features are perceptive nerve deafness and absence or delay in the development of speech, paralysis of the external rectus of one or both eyes, rectractio bulbi and features of the Klippel–Feil syndrome (extreme shortness and limited movement of the neck, due to fusing of the cervical vertebrae, and a low hairline).

The intelligence may vary from normal to the severely subnormal.

### b. **Mandibulo-facial Dyostosis (Berry–Franchescetti Syndrome)**

This syndrome is inherited in an autosomal dominant manner due to a gene of poor penetrance.

The face has a typical appearance, which has been variously described as bird-, fish- or sheep-like. This is due to gross underdevelopment of the bones of the cheek and chin. The mouth is enlarged, the palate is high and there may be a cleft palate and hare-lip. The teeth are malformed.

The eyes have an anti-mongoloid shape. There is a notch ('coloboma') at the outer end of the lower eyelid.

The ears are malformed, with a narrow external auditory meatus and malformation of the middle and inner ear, resulting in deafness. There is a blind fistula between the angle of the mouth and the ear.

The hair grows forwards onto the cheek in a tongue-like process from above the ear.

The height and head circumference are below average.

The degree of mental subnormality varies from the mild to the severe. The facial appearance and deafness often suggest a degree of mental subnormality much more severe than is, in fact, the case, if the effects of the patient's isolation can be overcome by operation or by special training for the deaf.

### c. Mandibulo-oculo-facial Dyscephaly (Hallerman–Streiff Syndrome)

This syndrome is inherited in an autosomal dominant manner.

The facial appearance is somewhat similar to that in mandibulo-facial dysotosis. As in the latter condition, the bones of the cheek and chin are underdeveloped, the palate is high and narrow and the teeth are malformed. In the present condition the nose is beaked and there is a double cutaneous chin with a central cleft.

The eyes are smaller than usual, and congenital cataracts, nystagmus and strabismus may be present.

The skin of the face is atrophic, particularly that of the nose. 'Alopecia areata' occurs in the scalp, eyebrows and eyelashes. The height and head circumference are below average.

The degree of mental subnormality varies from mild to severe.

### d. Rubinstein–Taybi's Syndrome

The evidence points to a genetic basis for this condition, although this is not yet proved.

The facial appearance is less abnormal than in the previously described first arch syndromes. The eyes have an anti-mongoloid slant, the nose is beaked and the palate high and narrow, but the bones of the cheek and chin are more normally developed. The ears are often of simple pattern and may be low-set or rotated. There may also be pigmented naevi of the forehead or sacrum and various skeletal abnormalities, but the feature by which the syndrome can be most easily recognized is the abnormal breadth of the thumbs and big toes.

The degree of mental subnormality is usually severe.

Dermatoglyphics have a high incidence of dermal ridge patterns on the thenar and hallucal areas, with a large loop opening into the first interdigital area in the latter case.

### e. Smith–Lemli–Opitz Syndrome

This condition is inherited in an autosomal recessive manner. Affected children have low birth weights, microcephaly and a characteristic facial appearance due to ptosis, a short nose with a flattened bridge and anteverted nostrils, and an underdeveloped chin.

30

Cleft palate and cardiac abnormalities are frequently present. There are simian creases on the palms and syndactyly of the toes. Hypospadias and cryptorchidism occur in males.

The degree of mental subnormality is usually severe but, on occasions, may be mild.

Dermatoglyphics show a high number of digital whorls and a reduced frequency of ulnar loops.

## 7. OTHER SYNDROMES OF GENETIC ORIGIN

In the following syndromes of genetic origin the facial appearance is less abnormal than in those previously described.

### a. Ataxia Telangiectasia (Louis–Bar Syndrome)

This condition is inherited in an autosomal recessive manner.

Affected children appear normal at birth, but between the ages of 3 and 5 years develop 'telangiectasia' (prominent dilated capillaries) on the conjunctiva of the eyeball, spreading to the eyelids, the face, ears and neck, the antecubital fossa, the wrists and hands, the popliteal fossa and sometimes the feet. There may also be *café-au-lait* spots and areas of depigmentation of the skin, and premature greying of the hair.

Signs of progressive cerebellar and extrapyramidal involvement appear concurrently with the skin lesions. The affected child becomes unsteady on his feet and his speech becomes slurred. His movements become incoordinated with an intention tremor and, eventually, choreo-athetosis, mask-like facies, limited eye movements and nystagmus.

Gradual mental deterioration occurs so that mental subnormality is obvious by the age of 9 years.

Due to a deficiency of the immunoglobulin IgA, affected children are very susceptible to infections of the lungs and upper respiratory tract. The thymus and lymphoid tissue generally are deficient and there is persistent lymphopenia in many cases and a tendency to develop neoplasms of lymphatic tissue.

There is no specific treatment for this condition and death usually occurs by the age of 20 years.

### b. Cerebro-metacarpo-metatarsal Dystrophy (Pseudo-pseudo-hypoparathyroidism, Albright's Syndrome)

The genetics of this condition are not clearly understood but it occurs four times as frequently in females as in males.

Persons affected are below average height and of obese or stocky build, with a broad or round face. The metacarpal and metatarsal bones are shorter than normal. As a result, when the fists are clenched, the metacarpophalangeal line has a characteristic appearance, being concave or straight rather than slightly convex. The nails are hypoplastic.

The serum calcium and phosphorus levels are normal. The EEG is abnormal.

The degree of mental subnormality is usually moderately severe.

Dermatoglyphics show a high incidence of arches in the finger tips.

### c. Laurence–Moon–Biedl Syndrome

This condition is inherited in an autosomal recessive manner. There is obesity of the Frölich type with hypogenitalism. Extra fingers and toes are present ('polydactyly'). The eyes show various abnormalities — 'retinitis pigmentosa' and often optic atrophy and nystagmus. ('Retinitis pigmentosa' is not, in fact, an inflammatory condition, but rather a degenerative process affecting the rods and cones; which is more accurately described by the term 'tapeto-retinal degeneration'.) Night vision is very poor and vision rapidly deteriorates.

Severe subnormality is obvious from infancy, but is not progressive.

Dermatoglyphics show an increased incidence of whorls on the finger tips and an extra digital triradius is often present.

### d. Tuberous Sclerosis (Epiloia)

This condition is inherited in an autosomal dominant manner, but the gene concerned has poor penetrance so that only partial features of the disease may occur. Its incidence has been estimated at between 1 in 100 000 and 1 in 300 000 live births.

In its fully developed form there are three cardinal signs: mental subnormality (usually severe), epilepsy and a facial rash ('adenoma sebaceum'), and an overgrowth of the sebaceous glands, which appears at about the fourth or fifth year of life and which, when fully developed, spreads out from the nose over each cheek in the form of a butterfly's wings and also onto the chin.

There may also be fibromata beneath the finger nails and on the back of the trunk and so-called 'shagreen patches'—raised, flat, thickened areas of skin—in the lumbosacral region, and the skin may show café-au-lait or white (depigmented) patches before the development of the facial rash. Flat, oval or circular greyish-white patches ('phakomata') may be seen in the retina.

Smooth muscle tumours may be present in the walls of the heart, and yellowish vascular tumours, consisting of a mixture of smooth muscle, blood vessels and fat, in the kidneys.

Throughout the substance of the brain, and often protruding into the ventricle, there are sclerotic nodules of varying size, consisting of localized overgrowths of neuroglia. These sometimes become calcified and may be visible in radiographs during life. Radiographs of the lungs may have a honeycomb appearance, due to the presence of many small cysts caused by the growth of multiple small, smooth muscle tumours from the walls of the smaller bronchi and blood vessels.

Various endocrine disturbances have been reported involving thyroid, pituitary–adrenal and carbohydrate metabolism.

The presence of cutaneous signs of the disease in either of the parents of a child with tuberosclerosis indicates that the parent is a heterozygote and that there is a 1 in 2 risk of another child being afflicted.

### e. Marinesco–Sjögren Syndrome

This conditions is inherited in an autosomal recessive manner.

Affected children are microcephalic and short in stature, with kyphosis, abnormalities of the ribs, broad fingers, talipes equinovarus and pes planus. The hair is scanty or absent and such hair as is present is fine, short and devoid of pigment. Strabismus and cataracts are present and blindness occurs early.

Cerebellar ataxia develops early in life with nystagmus, slurred speech, hypotonia, progressive motor weakness and convulsions.

The degree of mental subnormality is severe, but not progressive.

### 8. *X-LINKED DISORDERS*

Apart from those associated with the inborn metabolic disorders there are a number of genetically determined disorders associated with mental subnormality, which are inherited in a sex-linked or X-linked manner.

### a. Oculocerebral Degeneration (Norrie's Disease)

In this rare condition, males develop cataracts and blindness shortly after birth and the eyes degenerate and shrink in size during the first decade. The hearing may also be impaired and epilepsy may occur.

The degree of mental subnormality varies.

## b. Renpenning's Syndrome

The main characteristic of this syndrome is the normal physical appearance of the affected males. They are severely subnormal with IQs in the 35–50 range.

It has been suggested that Renpenning's syndrome may be responsible for the mental retardation of as many as 10 per cent of males in this IQ range.

## c. X-Linked Hydrocephalus

In affected males the aqueduct of Sylvius in the brain fails to develop fully and the cerebrospinal fluid accumulates in the ventricles. As a result, the skull becomes enlarged to a variable degree. This enlargement is characteristically globular, and, with the normal-sized face, gives the head the appearance of an inverted pyramid. There may be defects of vision and hearing. In X-linked hydrocephalus the skull and face are frequently asymmetrical. The thumbs are held flexed across the palms and there is spasticity of the legs.

The degree of mental subnormality is severe.

The prognosis and treatment of hydrocephalus will be referred to later.

## d. X-Linked Spastic Paraplegia

Affected males have a rather fixed facial expression. Nystagmus may be present even at rest, tongue movements are spastic, and the speech is slurred. Paresis and spasticity are more marked in the legs than in the arms, which show athetoid movements. Reflexes are increased and the plantar responses are extensor. It is unusual for wasting of the leg muscles to occur.

The degree of mental subnormality is severe.

## 9. SYNDROMES WITH A POSSIBLE GENETIC CAUSE

### a. 'Happy Puppet' Syndrome

The skull is microcephalic, with flattening and sometimes a horizontal depression in the occipital area. In the eye the choroid is incompletely developed, with optic atrophy. The chin is prominent and the tongue is protruded frequently. The bodily movements are jerky and resemble those of a puppet, with easily provoked and prolonged paroxysms of laughter, hence the name of this syndrome. There is weakness of the limbs and trunk.

Infantile spasms or major fits occur and wave and spike activity is present in electro-encephalograms. Air encephalograms show cerebral atrophy and ventricular dilatations.

34

The degree of mental subnormality is severe.

Steroids and anticonvulsants have produced limited improvement in some cases.

## b. de Lange Syndrome

Fetal movements are said to be reduced during pregnancy. At birth, affected children have a low weight for their maturity. Their condition is poor and they often fail to suck or cry. They have a characteristic facial appearance. The eyebrows are bushy and meet across the midline ('synophrys') and the eyelashes are long and curved. The hairline is low on the forehead and the face excessively hairy. The bridge of the nose is depressed and the nostrils face forward. The upper lip is elongated vertically and the mouth droops at the corners. The ears are low-set.

The hands, too, are characteristic. The thumb is proximally placed and, with the short, semi-flexed fingers, give the hand the appearance of a lobster's claw. More severe deformities of the hands may be present. The elbows cannot be fully extended. Deformities of the feet are less obvious. They tend to be short and to show fusion of the second and third toes ('syndactyly').

The trunk is excessively hairy and the external genitalia are under-developed.

The degree of mental subnormality is usually severe. Compulsive self-mutilating behaviour similar to that in the Lesch–Nyhan syndrome has been reported.

Dermatoglyphics are helpful in establishing the diagnosis. The fingerprint patterns show an increased frequency of radial loops and a decrease of whorls. The 'atd' angle is intermediate between normal and that in mongolism.

Cases of severe subnormality have been reported, in which the dwarfism and hirsutism of the de Lange syndrome are associated with dislocation of the radial heads at the elbow and absence of the fifth terminal phalanges, finger nails and toenails.

## c. Naevoid Amentia (Sturge–Weber Syndrome)

This is a fairly rare condition in which half of the face, neck and upper part of the chest is covered with a naevus—the so-called 'port-wine stain'. Hemiparesis is present, usually on the opposite side of the body, although both sides may be affected, and epileptic fits occur. The eye on the same side as the naevus is larger than that on the opposite side—'buphthalmos' or 'ox-eye'.

The facial naevus is associated with an angiomatous growth in the meninges on the corresponding side of the brain and adherent to it.

The degree of mental subnormality is usually severe and there may be marked behaviour disorders. The condition has been reported in persons of normal intelligence.

Marked improvement in behaviour and reduction in the frequency of fits sometimes follows operative removal of the meningeal naevus and part or all of the corresponding cerebral hemisphere.

### d. Prader–Willi Syndrome

Children with this syndrome are hypotonic from birth. In infancy, the facial appearance is said to be characteristic with the forehead seeming narrow, the eyes having an almond-shaped appearance and strabismus being present. These features become less obvious as the child becomes older, but the unusual smallness of the hands then becomes apparent. In males, hypogenitalism and cryptorchidism occur. By about the age of 2 years, excessive weight gain occurs and, by the age of 3 to 5 years, gross obesity is present which cannot be controlled by diets, and diabetes mellitus may develop.

The degree of mental subnormality may vary from mild to severe. Affected children are usually affectionate and stable until about 3 years of age, when they often become increasingly stubborn and are subject to temper tantrums. Serious personality disorders persist through adolescence and into adult life and take the form of outbursts of temper and violence with little provocation. Periods of depression may also occur.

It has been suggested that this syndrome may be the result of a developmental defect in the hypothalamus.

## 10. INBORN ERRORS OF METABOLISM ASSOCIATED WITH MENTAL SUBNORMALITY

About 80 inborn errors of metabolism known to cause mental subnormality have so far been reported. It was thought that they were due to single abnormal genes which each resulted in the absence of a single enzyme leading to the specific metabolic block concerned. It is now clear that each gene is responsible, not for a single enzyme, but for a polypeptide chain, and that the abnormal gene in any inborn metabolic error may exist in two or more different forms or 'alleles' and produce variations in the clinical manifestation of the disorder.

Most of the inborn errors of metabolism are inherited in an autosomal recessive manner but some as X-linked gene defects. A woman who is a carrier of a recessive gene runs a 1 in 100 risk of marrying a man who is the carrier of the same recessive gene, but if they are first cousins the risk is 1 in 8.

Few inborn metabolic errors can be detected by simple tests on the urine and the remainder require specialized pathological techniques including paper and gas chromatography for their detection. Reference will be made later to the antenatal diagnosis of these disorders.

## Disorders of Protein Metabolism

### Inborn Errors of Amino-acid Metabolism

PRIMARY OVERFLOW AMINO-ACIDURIAS

1. *Phenylketonuria*. At present this is the most common type of known metabolic error associated with mental subnormality, occurring once in about 12 000 live births. The autosomal recessive gene abnormality causes a deficiency of phenylalanine hydroxylase, the enzyme which takes part in the oxidation of the amino-acid phenylalanine to tyrosine, a precursor of the skin, hair and eye pigment, melanin. As a result of this deficiency there is an accumulation of phenylalanine in the blood and the excretion of phenylpyruvic acid in the urine, which is said to have a mousey smell.

The presence of phenylpyruvic acid in the urine may be detected by the ferric chloride and 'Phenistix' tests, but the former may give false-positive results and the latter may miss between a quarter and a half of affected children on routine testing between 4 and 6 weeks of age. More reliable is the Guthrie test, which depends on the ability of phenylalanine to promote the growth of *Bacillus subtilis* in the presence of an inhibitory substance in a culture medium. The size of the growth is directly related to the amount of phenylalanine present and this enables accurate quantitative estimations to be made. The test is carried out on filter paper impregnated with blood obtained from pricking a baby's heel between the ages of 6 and 14 days. Earlier testing may give misleadingly low levels in females. Not all babies with raised blood phenylalanine levels are suffering from phenylketonuria. This is the case with some premature babies in whom the serum tyrosine level also is raised initially, but will have returned to normal by the age of 2–3 weeks. Other babies with raised blood phenylalanine levels appear to have a high tolerance for this substance and do not show the classic clinical features of phenylketonuria or suffer brain damage. There is some recent evidence that it is the phenylalanine level in the granular white blood cells which is critical as regards mental development rather than the serum phenylalanine level. It is usual, however, to treat all babies whose blood phenylalanine exceeds 15 mg/100 ml. when fasting or after a normal meal or a phenylalanine loading test, or who excrete the characteristic metabolites in their urine when that blood level is exceeded.

Children with phenylketonuria have lower birth weights than their unaffected siblings. Because of the deficiency of melanin they are characteristically fair haired, fair skinned and blue eyed in the races

37

of Northern Europe and lighter in their colouring than their siblings in races with generally more marked pigmentation. They are prone to develop infantile eczema.

Phenylketonuria, if untreated, is always associated with some degree of mental subnormality, usually severe, but occasionally very mild. There is, however, no progressive mental deterioration in this condition. About half the affected children never learn to talk and about a third never learn to walk. They sometimes show autistic features, not relating to other people, and resisting cuddling, but becoming unusually attached to small objects. They frequently show mannerisms such as posturing with the hands and rocking backwards and forwards for hours on end.

Between a quarter and a third of patients with phenylketonuria suffer from epilepsy, usually of the grand mal type, but this tends to disappear with age. In the majority of cases there are minor abnormalities in the EEG and also an increased frequency in their near relatives.

The development of mental subnormality in children in whom phenylketonuria is detected can be prevented by feeding them from birth with diets in which the amount of phenylalanine is restricted so that serum levels are between 2·5 mg and 10 mg per cent, and to which tyrosine and vitamin supplements have been added. The child's progress has to be carefully monitored and its diet adjusted if necessary. If the phenylalanine intake is restricted too severely the child may become fretful, lose its appetite, may vomit and its physical and mental growth are retarded. It may develop a severe rash which fails to respond to all local treatment. Phenylketonuric children on phenylalanine-restricted diets gain weight less rapidly than phenylketonuric children on unrestricted diets.

It has been suggested that, after the age of 3, the brain may be capable of withstanding the harmful effects of raised levels of phenylalanine in the blood so that a return to a normal diet may be made after that age. However, successfully treated phenylketonuric women may have to return to their special diets during pregnancy if damage to the brain of a non-phenylketonuric fetus is to be avoided. Similarly, women who are carriers of the gene for phenylketonuria may have levels of phenylalanine in the blood raised sufficiently to cause fetal damage and may require phenylalanine-restricted diets during pregnancy. A significantly increased percentage of Rhesus-negative women has been reported among the mothers of phenylketonuric children.

Reproduction in successfully treated phenylketonurics carries with it the theoretical possibility of a gradually increasing number of carriers of the gene for phenylketonuria and a consequent increase in the number of sufferers from this condition. This possibility underlines the need for genetic counselling in this and all other abnormal conditions with a known genetic basis.

2. *Homocystinuria.* At present homocystinuria would appear to be the second most common inborn error of amino-acid metabolism known to cause mental subnormality, occurring about a quarter as frequently as phenylketonuria. It is inherited in an autosomal recessive manner and results in deficiency of the enzyme cystathionine synthetase, which normally takes part in the conversion of the amino-acid methionine to cystine. In homocystinuria the process is arrested at the stage between homocystine and cystathionine. The levels of both methionine and homocystine are raised in the blood, and homocystine is excreted in the urine, which is said to have a sulphurous odour. Homocystine may be detected in the urine by the cyanide nitroprusside test.

The physical signs of homocystinuria are fair hair and skin, dislocation of the lenses of the eyes, a characteristic flush of the cheeks, enlarged joints, knock-knees and a shuffling gait. The peripheral circulation is poor, with well-marked livido reticularis and a tendency for various thromboembolic phenomena to occur. These signs of homocystinuria are not obvious at birth and, as the child becomes older, osteoporosis may occur and the skeletal abnormalities may become more marked and resemble those of Marfan's Syndrome, in which mental subnormality is rare, with a high arched palate, chest deformities and long narrow fingers. The liver undergoes fatty degeneration and fits are frequent. Early mental development is usually normal but signs of gross deterioration appear in the most severe cases in the first year of life. It is more common for mental deterioration to become obvious at about the time of starting school but homocystinuria is not incompatible with normal intelligence in adult life. Homocystinuria may sometimes present with schizophrenia-like symptoms.

The development of mental subnormality may be prevented by treatment with a diet low in methionine and supplemented with cystine. A proportion of cases respond to the administration of pyridoxine without the necessity for these dietary restrictions. In such cases there appears to be no deficiency of cystathionine synthetase.

3. *Argininosuccinic Aciduria.* This condition is inherited in an autosomal recessive manner. There is a deficiency of the enzyme arginosuccinase, which normally takes part in the conversion of the amino-acid argininosuccinic acid into arginine and fumaric acid. As a result argininosuccinic acid accumulates in the blood and appears in the urine. Blood ammonia levels are also raised. Argininosuccinic aciduria may be detected by enzyme estimations in amniotic cell cultures and carriers may be detected by argininosuccinase estimations in their red blood cells.

The most striking physical signs in this condition are related to the absence of arginine, which is normally present in hair. The hair is abnormally brittle, so that its length never exceeds 5–10 mm. On examination each hair shows irregularly alternating spindle-like swellings and strictures ('monilethrix'). The nails, also, may be brittle and various skin disorders may be present. Affected children show an early refusal to eat protein and develop clonic spasms and convulsions and later choreiform movements and mild ataxia.

The degree of mental subnormality may be severe, but in mild examples of this condition the hair abnormalities may be the only sign of the disorder.

Treatment consists of restricting the protein intake, but results have, so far, been disappointing.

Monilethrix occurs also in Menkes' syndrome ('kinky hair disease'), which is inherited in an X-linked manner. Affected male infants fail to thrive. They are microcephalic, with micrognathia and a high arched palate. The hair on the scalp is sparse, coarse, stubbly, kinky and white, due to absence of pigment.

The degree of mental subnormality is severe, and progressive mental deterioration occurs, with convulsions, increasing spasticity, and death in a state of decerebrate rigidity by the age of about 3 years.

The nature of the underlying metabolic disorder is not known but paper chromatography has shown an increase in glutamic acid in some cases.

4. *Arginaemia*. This condition is very much rarer than arginino-succinic aciduria and its mode of inheritance is not known with certainty. It is due to a deficiency of the enzyme arginase, which is responsible for the metabolism of arginine, which accumulates in the blood in this condition. The blood ammonia levels are also raised.

Affected children have spastic paraplegia and convulsions and are severely subnormal.

In spite of its apparent rarity this condition is of particular interest in view of the possibility of its effective treatment, not by dietary restrictions as in other inborn metabolic errors, but by the replacement of the missing enzyme, arginase. Arginase is synthesized by the Shope papilloma virus, which is harmless to man. It has been injected into two sisters suffering from arginaemia in the hope of overcoming the metabolic block and reducing their blood arginine levels to normal.

5. *Citrullinuria*. It is probable that this, so far very rare condition, is inherited in an autosomal recessive manner. Due to the deficiency of the enzyme argininosuccinic acid synthetase, citrulline accumulates in the blood and appears in the urine with a number of other amino-acids in considerably increased concentrations.

The condition manifests itself during the first year of life in attacks of vomiting, generalized convulsions, arrested development and subsequent regression to a severely subnormal level, with marked irritability.

So far no treatment has been devised to prevent the mental deterioration, but vomiting and convulsions may cease and the child become more responsive and less irritable if the protein in his diet is restricted.

6. *Cystathioninuria.* It is probable that this condition is inherited in an autosomal recessive manner, but it has been suggested that it may be caused by a dominant gene of variable penetrance. Cystathionine, like homocystine, is an intermediate product in the conversion of methionine to cystine, but in cystathioninuria the block is at a later stage of the metabolic process. The block is due to a deficiency of the enzyme cystathionase. Cystathionine accumulates in the blood and appears in the urine.

The growth of affected children is arrested and they tend to be anaemic and to have persistent thrombocytopenia. The degree of mental subnormality varies widely in individual cases.

Treatment consists of administering pyridoxine, which increases the growth rate and reduces, if not prevents, the degree of mental subnormality. To protect the developing fetus, mothers who are heterozygous for this condition should be given pyridoxine throughout their pregnancies.

7. *Histidinaemia.* This condition is inherited in an autosomal recessive manner. There is a deficiency of the enzyme histidine ammonia lyase, which is necessary for the conversion of histidine to urocanic acid, a precursor of glutamic acid. Histidine accumulates in the blood and it appears in the urine with considerable amounts of imidazole pyruvic acid and imidazole acetic acid. The importance of imidazole pyruvic acid is that it may give a false-positive reaction to the 'Phenistix' and ferric chloride tests and lead to errors in diagnosis.

Many of the affected children are fair-haired and blue-eyed. The degree of mental impairment varies considerably. Some cases are severely subnormal, others are within the normal range of intelligence, but all have in common speech defects.

Treatment consists of restricting the amount of histidine in the diet, from early infancy onwards, so as to minimize the risk of inevitable brain damage and mental impairment.

8. *Hydroxykynureninuria.* The mode of inheritance of this disorder is not known with certainty. There is a deficiency of the enzyme kynureninase, which is necessary for the conversion of kynurenine to 3-hydroxy-anthranilic acid, a precursor of nicotinic acid. As a result, there are signs of nicotinic acid deficiency and growth is stunted.

The degree of mental subnormality may be only slight and some cases may be normal in intelligence.

Treatment with large doses of pyridoxine, with nicotinic acid supplements, may improve the physical condition, but the effect on the mental condition is uncertain.

9. *Hydroxylysinuria.* The mode of inheritance and the nature of the metabolic disorder in this condition are not fully understood. The level of hydroxylisine is raised in the blood and urine.

Affected children tend to be hyperactive and to have myoclonic and major motor seizures. Their degree of mental subnormality is severe.

No effective treatment of this condition is known.

10. *Hydroxyprolinaemia.* The mode of inheritance and the nature of the metabolic disorder in this condition are not yet fully understood, but it is known to be associated with a deficiency of the enzyme hydroxyproline oxidase.

Affected children are retarded in their development and suffer from attacks of haematuria. They are severely subnormal and hyperactive.

No effective treatment of this condition is known.

11. *Hyperammonaemia.* This condition is inherited in an autosomal recessive manner. It is a disorder of the urea cycle, due to a deficiency of the enzyme ornithine transcarbamylase, leading to an accumulation of ammonia in the blood.

Symptoms appear when the child is weaned from breast to cow's milk, at which time it develops anorexia and starts to vomit. At first irritable, it later becomesl ethargic and develops convulsions and has episodes of extreme muscular rigidity with intermittent opisthotonus. The liver becomes progressively enlarged.

The degree of mental subnormality is severe.

Treatment consists of limiting the daily protein intake to less than 1·5 g per kg body weight, in frequent small feeds.

12. *Hyperglycinaemia.* This condition is probably inherited in an autosomal recessive manner. The exact nature of the metabolic disorder in this condition is not known, but the level of glycine in the blood is raised and it appears in the urine with increased amounts of glyoxylic acid and oxalic acid.

Affected children are retarded in their growth and develop epilepsy shortly after birth.

The degree of mental subnormality is severe.

Treatment with a protein-restricted diet reduces the frequency of the fits and prolongs the child's life, but mental subnormality may not be prevented.

13. *Hyperlysinaemia.* This condition is inherited in an autosomal recessive manner. There is a deficiency of the enzyme lysine-keto-glutamate reductase, resulting in an increase in the amount of lysine

in both blood and urine, and the amount of other amino-acids is also increased in the urine. The blood ammonia level rises.

Affected children have feeding difficulties due to impaired swallowing. The liver and spleen enlarge progressively. The hair is brittle. Severe convulsions occur with hypertonia and flexion spasms in between. The degree of mental subnormality varies. There is no known effective treatment.

14. *Hyperprolinaemia.* The mode of inheritance and the nature of the metabolic disorder in this condition are not yet fully understood, but it is known to be associated with a deficiency of the enzyme proline oxidase.

Early development is usually normal and then feeding difficulties occur and frequent generalized convulsions develop. Marked deafness is present, and persistent haematuria and attacks of pyuria occur in association with defective renal development. The EEG is abnormally sensitive to photic stimulation.

Mental development varies from severe subnormality to superior intelligence.

No effective treatment of this condition is known.

15. *Hypervalinaemia.* It is probable that this condition is inherited in an autosomal recessive manner. There is a deficiency of the enzyme valine transaminase, which is necessary for the conversion of lysine to alpha-keto-isovaleric acid.

Affected children have difficulty in sucking, have attacks of vomiting and fail to thrive. Blindness may occur. The degree of mental subnormality is variable.

A diet in which the amounts of valine, leucine and isoleucine are restricted may improve the physical condition, but its effect on the mental state is uncertain.

16. *Maple Syrup Urine Disease.* This disease is so called because of the characteristic smell of the urine, which is said to resemble that of maple syrup. Its frequency has been estimated at about 1 per 250 000 live births. It is inherited in an autosomal recessive manner.

There is a deficiency of the enzyme ketoacid decarboxylase, causing a disturbance of the metabolism of the branched-chain amino-acids (BCAA) valine, leucine, isoleucine and allo-isoleucine, which are present in the blood and urine in abnormal amounts. The reaction of the urine to the ferric chloride test may be mistaken for that of phenylketonuria, but the two conditions may be clearly differentiated by paper chromatography.

Maple syrup disease manifests itself in the first week of life. The infant becomes irritable, has difficulty in sucking and swallowing and breathes in a jerky manner. If untreated, signs of progressive cerebral involvement occur: convulsions, paralyses, rigidity and opisthotonus, leading to death in a few months.

There is an intermittent form of this disease, in which the typical urine is excreted only during infections and in which the degree of mental subnormality may be minimal or absent.

Treatment consists of a synthetic diet containing the minimum amounts of leucine, isoleucine and valine necessary to maintain their normal levels in the blood. Very early diagnosis is essential for treatment to be effective. As with any other synthetic diet, growth may be retarded. Some cases respond to thiamine hydrochloride without any dietary restrictions.

17. *Oculocerebro-renal Syndrome* (*Lowe's Syndrome*). It is probable that this condition is inherited in an X-linked manner. The exact nature of the metabolic disorder is not known, but there is a decreased ability of the renal tubules to regulate the acid–base balance, with resulting acidosis.

A number of amino-acids are excreted in the urine, but the paper chromatography pattern is not specific.

Affected children develop anorexia, and growth is severely retarded, with osteomalacia and, later, rickets developing. Cataracts are present from birth and there is generalized hypotonia. Cryptorchidism is a common feature. Affected children are said to have a characteristic appearance, with a dome-shaped head with frontal bossing and large eyes sunk well into their sockets. The thoracic diameter is increased and the upper abdomen is protuberant due to the chronic hyperventilation provoked by the acidosis.

Many affected children die in early infancy. Those that survive are severely subnormal. There is no effective treatment of the underlying biochemical disorder, but in some cases the resulting rickets may be successfully treated with vitamin D and alkali, and these cases may survive into early childhood.

18. *Ornithinaemia.* The mode of inheritance of this condition is not known with certainty. It is due to a deficiency of the enzyme ornithine keto-acid transaminase, which is responsible for the metabolism of ornithine to γ-glutamylsemialdehyde, a precursor of glutamic acid. As a result there is an increase in the level of ornithine in the blood and a marked generalized amino-aciduria, especially of proline and valine, but not of ornithine. Glycosuria occurs due to renal tubular damage.

Affected children fail to thrive during infancy and are retarded in their development of speech. They develop cirrhosis of the liver.

The degree of mental subnormality may vary from the severe to the mild.

The effectiveness of treatment by restricting the ornithine intake is not yet proved.

19. *Ornithine Transcarbamylase Deficiency.* The mode of inheritance of this condition is not known with certainty, but there is some

evidence that it may be X-linked. As a result of the deficiency of the enzyme ornithine transcarbamylase the synthesis of citrulline is defective. Ammonia accumulates in the blood.

Affected children are retarded in their growth and subject to attacks of vomiting and screaming and, later, lethargy and stupor. The development of speech is delayed.

The degree of mental subnormality is severe.

Treatment consists of limiting the dietary protein and giving citric acid and aspartic acid supplements in order to reduce the blood ammonia levels and minimize the degree of brain damage.

20. *Tryptophanuria.* The mode of inheritance of this condition is not known with certainty, nor is the exact nature of the metabolic disorder. The level of tryptophan is raised in both blood and urine.

Affected children are retarded in their growth, and hyperpigmentation and thickening of the skin develops by about the sixth month.

The degree of mental subnormality is severe.

There is no known effective treatment.

RENAL (TRANSPORT) AMINO-ACIDURIAS

1. *Hartnup Disease.* This condition is inherited in an autosomal recessive manner. There is a deficit in the transport of amino-acids across the mucous membranes of the intestines and across the epithelium of the renal tubules. In particular, tryptophan absorption is grossly defective and results in a deficiency of nicotinic acid, of which it is a precursor. There is an abnormal excretion in the urine of a number of amino-acids, which produce a characteristic pattern on paper chromatography. The urine always contains also a large amount of indole-3-acetic acid and usually a large amount of indican. There is a moderate increase of protoporphyrin in the faeces.

The most constant clinical feature of this condition is photosensitivity, with the development of a rash identical with that in pellagra on exposure to the sun, i.e. there is roughening, reddening and, in some cases, cracking and ulceration of the skin of the exposed areas of the body, raised above and sharply defined from the unaffected skin.

In untreated cases there is a great loss of weight, and the neurological signs of pellagra may occur, with mental confusion and ataxia prominent. Diarrhoea is not a constant feature.

Children in whom the metabolic abnormality is present are mentally subnormal to varying degrees, even if the obvious 'pellagroid' signs are not present. The neurological and skin signs dramatically disappear and the weight returns to normal with the administration of large doses of nicotinamide, but there is no improvement in intelligence and the abnormal excretion of amino-acids persists.

2. *Methionine Malabsorption (Oast House Urine) Syndrome.* It is thought that this condition is inherited in an autosomal recessive manner. The primary disorder is an inability to absorb methionine from the gut. Bacterial fermentation of methionine then occurs and leads to an accumulation of the keto-acids and hydroxy-acids of phenylalanine, tyrosine, leucine and methionine in the blood and their excretion in the urine, which has a smell said to resemble that of beer, dry celery or burnt sugar.

Affected children have feeding difficulties and fail to thrive. They resemble children with phenylketonuria in having fair hair and blue eyes. They suffer from attacks of diarrhoea and convulsions.

The degree of mental subnormality is severe.

Early treatment with a methionine-restricted diet may improve the physical condition and prevent the development of mental subnormality.

### Disorders of Carbohydrate Metabolism

1. *Galactosaemia*

This condition is inherited in an autosomal recessive manner. There is a deficiency or absence of the enzyme phosphogalactose uridyl transferase, which is necessary for the conversion of galactose-1-phosphate to glucose. As a result, there is an accumulation of galactose and galactose-1-phosphate in the blood, which damages the liver and kidneys, and galactose appears in the urine, as well as a number of amino-acids. The enzyme deficiency may be detected by estimations on amniotic cell cultures, but there is no simple routine ward test which is specific for the presence of galactose in the urine.

In severe cases symptoms appear in the first 2 weeks of life. The infant starts to vomit and becomes increasingly lethargic and reluctant to feed, loses weight and becomes jaundiced. If the condition is untreated, cirrhosis of the liver and cataracts develop and the child is severely subnormal and death occurs early. However, if the condition is diagnosed and treated shortly after birth by a galactose-free diet, the cataracts disappear, liver function returns to normal and the severity of mental subnormality may be reduced, if not entirely prevented.

2. *Glycogen Storage Disorders*

This group of disorders is inherited in an autosomal recessive manner. In most members of the group, hypoglycaemia occurs, due either to an inability to form normal glycogen or to convert stored glycogen into glucose. For some disorders in this group there is no known treatment and death occurs in infancy or early childhood, but in the following the child may survive long enough for his mental condition to cause concern:

## a. 'DEBRANCHER' DEFICIENCY

This condition is so called because there is a deficiency of the enzyme amylo-1,6-glucosidase, which is necessary for the breakdown of glycogen to glucose at the stage of cleavage at the points at which the glycogen molecule branches. As a result, abnormal glycogen accumulates in the tissues and blood levels of glucose are inadequate. The hypoglycaemia is increased in this condition because there is also a deficiency of the liver enzyme glucose-6-phosphatase, which is necessary for the release of glucose from glucose-6-phosphate.

Affected children have poor appetites and fail to thrive, so that growth is retarded and bone maturation is delayed. The liver becomes greatly enlarged and there are signs of malnutrition and emaciation. Recurrent respiratory infections occur. Convulsions, brain damage and severe subnormality result from the prolonged hypoglycaemia.

Glucose-6-phosphatase activity may be increased by the administration of triamcinolone, but there is no known way of increasing amylo-1,6-glucosidase activity.

## b. GLYCOGENOSIS

It is believed that this condition is due to a deficiency of the enzyme phosphorylase kinase, which is responsible for activating the liver enzyme phosphorylase. As a result, excessive amounts of abnormal glycogen accumulate in the liver and brain, and it is this that causes the damage rather than hypoglycaemia, which does not occur in this condition.

Affected children fail to thrive and are obviously retarded in reaching their developmental milestones. The liver becomes enlarged, cataracts may occur, and there are convulsions, signs of progressive brain damage, such as ataxia, nystagmus and cerebral palsy, with severe mental subnormality.

It is possible that early treatment with glucagon might diminish the degree of brain damage by preventing excessive glycogen deposition.

## 3. *Hypoglycemosis (or Idiopathic Hypoglycaemia)*

It is now thought that this condition is inherited in an autosomal dominant manner. Affected individuals have an abnormal sensitivity to leucine, which produces a rapid and prolonged fall in blood glucose and an excessive rise in plasma insulin.

Affected children develop convulsions in infancy and irreversible brain damage and severe subnormality, if prolonged hypoglycaemia is not treated early. Treatment consists of restricting leucine in the diet and giving extra glucose between feeds. ACTH may be necessary in severe cases. Fortunately, the leucine sensitivity is self-limiting and, by the age of 5 years, it may be possible for the child to resume a normal unrestricted diet.

### 4. *Familial Lactic Acidosis*

The mode of inheritance and the exact nature of the underlying metabolic disorder in this condition are not known with certainty. There is both an excessive production of lactic acid by erythrocytes and muscles and a deficient ability to metabolize it normally, with a resultant accumulation in the blood.

The condition manifests itself in the second year of life as attacks of hypernoea at rest, muscular twitching, progressive ataxia, convulsions, and mental deterioration, leading to death in about 6 months.

There is as yet no known specific treatment.

### Disorders of Lipid Metabolism

In this group of metabolic disorders there is abnormal storage of lipids in the tissues leading to their degeneration.

### 1. *Cerebromacular Degeneration* (*Amaurotic Familial Idiocy*)

Disorders in this rare group are inherited in an autosomal recessive manner and are characterized clinically by progressive mental and visual deterioration.

#### a. SPHINGOLIPIDOSES

i. *Tay–Sachs' Disease*. This condition is due to a deficiency of the enzyme hexosaminadase A, which results in an accumulation of ganglioside GM2 in the tissues. It occurs most frequently in Ashkenazi Jews, in whom the carrier rate is as high as 1 in 25. The onset is during the first year of life, often as early as the third month, and the course of the disease is progressive mental deterioration, blindness, convulsions and death within 2 years. Optic atrophy occurs, with the pathognomonic 'cherry-red spot' at the macula lutea. Hearing, however, remains acute until the terminal stages of the disease. There is progressive spastic paralysis affecting all muscles with, in some cases, a condition of decerebral rigidity just before death.

This disease occurs also both in a late infantile, and in a juvenile form, in which the onset may be delayed until the fifth to seventh year of life in children whose previous development has been normal.

The subsequent course is similar to that of the infantile form, although slower, with death occurring usually between the ages of 14 and 18 years.

There is no known treatment for this disease, but its incidence may be reduced by the termination of pregnancies in which a deficiency of hexosaminadase A is found in fibroblast cultures from amniotic fluid, and by the detection of carriers whose blood shows a similar, but less severe, deficiency of the enzyme.

ii. *Niemann–Pick Disease.* This condition is due to a deficiency of the enzyme sphingomyelinase, which is necessary for the normal break-down of sphingomyelin, which accumulates in excess in the tissues in this disease.

The onset and course of the disease are similar to those in Tay–Sachs' disease. As in that disease, the 'cherry-red spot' is present, but in addition there is marked enlargement of the liver and spleen, with pigmentation of the skin. This enlargement is due to infiltration with Niemann–Pick cells, which spread to all the organs in the body.

There is no known treatment of this disease, but antenatal diagnosis and the detection of carriers are possible by enzyme estimation.

iii. *Generalized Gangliosidosis.* In this condition there is a deficiency of the enzyme GMI ganglioside β-galactosidase, which results in an accumulation of GMI ganglioside in the brain, liver, spleen and kidneys.

The onset and course of this disease is similar to that of the late infantile form of Tay–Sachs' disease, with death occurring within the first 2 years of life.

There is no known treatment, but antenatal diagnosis and the detection of carriers are possible by enzyme estimations.

### b. NEURONAL CEROID-LIPOFUCINOSES

This group of disorders is inherited in an autosomal recessive manner and has in common the presence of large amounts of yellow brown granules, which appear to be a type of ceroid-lipofuscin pigment, in the cells of the brain and retina, which degenerate as a result. The nature of the underlying biochemical disorder is not known.

The late juvenile (Bielchowsky–Jansky disease) and juvenile (Batten–Vogt disease or Spielmeyer–Sjögren disease) forms are associated with mental subnormality.

i. *Bielchowsky–Jansky Disease.* The onset is between the ages of 1 and 4 years, with severe convulsions, signs of cerebellar dysfunction, optic atrophy and mental deterioration, with death within a few years.

ii. *Batten–Vogt Disease; Spielmeyer–Sjögren Disease.* In this disease the onset is between the ages of 5 and 10 years, and its progress is slower, with retinitis pigmentosa and visual loss, spasticity, extra-pyramidal signs, mental deterioration and the late onset of convulsions.

There is no known treatment for either of these diseases.

## 2. Cerebrosidoses

### a. GAUCHER'S DISEASE

This condition is inherited in an autosomal recessive manner. There is a deficiency of the enzyme cerebroside β-glucosidase, which results in an accumulation of various cerebrosides (Gaucher cells) in the brain, liver, spleen and other tissues of the body, including the bone marrow.

The onset of this condition is within the first 6 months of life, with signs of rapid deterioration of the brain and mental deterioration, with death at about the age of 1 year in a state of decerebrate rigidity.

There is no known treatment of this disease, but the enzyme deficiency may be detected in fibroblast cultures obtained by amniocentesis and by blood level estimations on carriers.

### b. METACHROMATIC LEUCODYSTROPHY

This condition is inherited in an autosomal recessive manner. There is a deficiency of the enzyme cerebroside sulphate sulphatase, which is necessary for the breakdown of sulphatide(ceramide-galactose-3-sulphate), a normal component of myelin. As a result of the deficiency there is a progressive accumulation of sulphatide in both the grey and white matter of the brain, in the peripheral nerve tissue, liver, gall bladder and kidney, and metachromatic granules appear in various tissues and in the urine. Myelin degeneration is followed by axon degeneration and neuroglial overgrowth.

The onset is usually after the first year of life and the course is marked by slowly progressive failure of hearing, speech and vision, muscular incoordination, epilepsy, mental deterioration and spastic paralysis, leading to decerebrate rigidity and death within 5–10 years.

There is no known treatment of this disease, but antenatal diagnosis and the detection of carriers is possible by enzyme estimations.

## 3. Refsum's Disease

This condition is inherited in an autosomal recessive manner. There is a deficiency of the enzyme phytanic acid oxidase, as a result of which there is a failure to convert phytol (a major constituent of the chlorophyll molecule) to carbon dioxide and an accumulation of the intermediate metabolite phytanic acid in many tissues, including the brain and the peripheral nerves. This leads to defective synthesis of myelin, a gradual loss of the myelin sheath and perineural fibrosis.

The onset may occur in childhood, when there may be progressive failure of vision, associated with retinitis pigmentosa and progressive nerve deafness. Ataxia, nystagmus and other cerebellar signs develop. Symmetrical weakness of the distal parts of the limbs occurs, with weakness of the deep reflexes.

Mental development is arrested and followed by varying degrees of mental deterioration.

In addition to the signs of damage to the central nervous system, ichthyosis (scaliness of the skin) occurs.

The degree of mental and physical deterioration may be reduced by giving a phytanic acid-free diet with vitamin A and E supplements.

Antenatal diagnosis and the detection of carriers are possible by enzyme estimations.

## Disorders of Connective Tissue

### 1. *Mucopolysaccharidoses*

Six different types are described in this group of disorders and are designated as MPS Types I–VI. Only in Types I–III is mental subnormality a constant feature. In each, abnormal storage of mucopolysaccharides occurs in the connective tissues, which undergo degeneration. It has been suggested that there is a link between the mucopolysaccharidoses and the lipidoses.

### a. MUCOPOLYSACCHARIDOSIS TYPE I (HURLER'S SYNDROME—GARGOYLISM)

This condition is inherited in an autosomal recessive manner. The exact nature of the enzyme defect is not known, but large quantities of chondroitin sulphate B and heparitin sulphate are excreted in the urine.

The physical signs of this condition are not obvious at birth, but develop during the first year of life. By this time the facial appearance is characteristic and is said to resemble that of a gargoyle. The head is large and may be generally misshapen, but typically there is frontal bossing, with prominent supra-orbital ridges and a depressed bridge of the nose. The sella turcica is elongated. The eyebrows are coarse and bushy, the ears are set low, the tongue is large, fissured and constantly protruded. The dentition is delayed and irregular. About 75 per cent of these patients show various degrees of corneal opacity, and defects of ocular movements and of balance are common. The neck is short and thick and the dorsal spine kyphotic owing to abnormal vertebral growth, which produces a characteristic 'beaked' appearance on radiographic examination. The centres of ossification

51

are delayed and the patient is short of stature and the limbs are relatively short, with limitation of extension of the joints.

The liver and spleen are greatly enlarged, with distension of the abdomen and often umbilical hernia. Congenital cardiac lesions are often present.

Mental development is arrested and the child undergoes progressive mental and physical deterioration and dies early in the second decade.

There is no known treatment, but the excess of heparitin sulphate and the presence of metachromatic granules in cells may be detected during pregnancy by aminocentesis and the possibility of termination of pregnancy considered.

### b. MUCOPOLYSACCHARIDOSIS TYPE II (HUNTER'S SYNDROME— GARGOYLISM)

This condition is inherited in an X-linked manner, and is about one-fifth as common as Hurler's syndrome. As in that condition, the exact nature of the enzyme defect is not known, and large quantities of chondroitin sulphate B and heparitin sulphate are excreted in the urine. The facial appearance is similar in the two conditions, but in Hunter's syndrome corneal clouding does not occur, but nerve deafness is present in about 40 per cent of cases, and dwarfing is less common than in Hurler's syndrome.

Mental deterioration occurs more slowly than in Hurler's syndrome.

There is no known treatment of Hunter's syndrome, but the excess of heparitin sulphate may be detected during pregnancy by amniocentesis and the possibility of termination of pregnancy considered. Carriers may be detected by the presence of metachromatic granules in cultured skin fibroblasts.

### c. MUCOPOLYSACCHARIDOSIS TYPE III (SANFILIPPO SYNDROME)

This condition is inherited in an autosomal recessive manner. The exact nature of the enzyme defect is not known, but large amounts of heparitin sulphate are excreted in the urine. The physical signs of this disease are less marked than those in Hurler's and Hunter's syndromes. The skull is obviously enlarged and very thick, and deafness frequently occurs. There is moderate dwarfing, the joints are stiffened and the liver may be moderately enlarged. In contrast to the mildness of the physical signs, the degree of mental subnormality is severe, with considerable intellectual deterioration by the age of 5.

There is no known treatment for this condition, but the excess of heparitin sulphate may be detected during pregnancy by amniocentesis and the possibility of termination of pregnancy considered.

# Other Inborn Errors of Metabolism

## 1. *Glucose-6-phosphate-dehydrogenase* (*G6PD*) *Deficiency*

This condition occurs most frequently in Negro races in whom it is inherited in an X-linked manner. As a result of the deficiency of G6PD, affected males are predisposed to develop an haemolytic anaemia when drugs such as aspirin, sulphonamides or some anti-malarial drugs are administered. The resulting damage to the brain may be sufficient to cause mental subnormality. The jaundice may be present at birth if the mother has taken such drugs during pregnancy. Further brain damage may be prevented by avoiding the administration of the types of drugs mentioned.

## 2. *Hepatolenticular Degeneration* (*Wilson's Disease*)

This condition is inherited in an autosomal recessive manner. It is a disorder of copper metabolism in which there is both excessive absorption of copper from the diet and a deficiency of the normal copper-carrying protein, caeruloplasmin. As a result, there is greatly increased excretion of copper in the urine, with renal damage and a generalized amino-aciduria, proteinuria and glycosuria.

The signs of hepatolenticular degeneration occur most frequently in the second decade, in a child who has previously been mentally normal, but who may have failed to thrive and suffered from jaundice. Involuntary choreiform movements with tremor develop and there is progressive difficulty in articulation and in swallowing. Rigidity of the muscles of the limbs, trunk and face occurs, followed by contractures and gradual muscle wasting.

The physical signs are associated with degeneration in the lenticular nuclei of the brain, due to copper deposition and grossly disturbed function of the liver, which develops polylobular cirrhosis from the same cause.

A smoky brownish ring ('Kayser-Fleischer ring'), due to deposits of copper at the outer margin of the cornea, is pathognomonic of this condition, and so-called 'sunflower cataracts', due to copper deposits in the lens capsule, are rare accompaniments.

Hyperpigmentation may occur on the front of the legs, due to the increased deposition of melanin in the basal layer of the epididymis, possibly as the result of the disturbed liver function.

If untreated, there is progressive mental deterioration, and paranoid psychosis with hallucinations may occur. Emaciation in the acute form leads to death in 3–7 years. Early treatment may prevent physical and mental deterioration. Treatment is directed at reducing the absorption of copper by limiting it in the diet and by administering potassium sulphide, and by mobilizing the excess copper from the tissues to be excreted in the urine by administering the chelating agents D-penicillamine and dimercaprol. The use of L-dopa and triethylene tetramine dihydrochloride has been claimed to be effective in cases where the other chelating agents fail.

### 3. *Hypothyroidism* (*Cretinism*)

It is now believed that as many as five distinct inborn metabolic errors may cause the clinical picture of this condition. All result in a deficiency of the thyroid gland secretion, thyroxine. The mode of inheritance is not known with certainty, but in three it is believed to be in an autosomal recessive manner. Thyroxine obtained from the mother during pregnancy is sufficient to prevent the signs of the condition manifesting themselves at birth, but insufficient to protect the fetal brain and skeleton completely from the effects of lack of thyroxine. Unfortunately, if diagnosis and treatment are delayed until after the age of 3 months, the chances of preventing irreparable brain damage become progressively less.

Early clinical signs are apathy and lethargy in feeding, partly due to enlargement of the tongue, which also causes noisy breathing. Frequently, the feeding problems are the only complaints about the baby the mother may have at this stage. If untreated, the baby becomes increasingly slow and does not readily laugh or smile. The skin becomes yellowish, loose and wrinkled, with marked puffiness of the skin and thickening of the eyelids, nostrils, lips, feet and back of the neck, which is short and thick. Fatty pads develop above the clavicles, in the axillae and between the scapulae. The abdomen becomes protuberant and umbilical hernia may occur. The hair of the head and eyebrows is scanty. The temperature is subnormal and the baby emits a characteristic leathery cry.

Later, the baby makes no attempt to sit up, stand or walk at the normal ages. The epiphyses are delayed in their appearance, growth is stunted and the anterior fontanelle may still be open in adult life. Speech may not appear until as late as 7 or 8 years of age. Sexual development may be delayed or incomplete.

In untreated cases there is inevitably mental subnormality. The institution of treatment after the age of 3 months may allow mental and physical development to progress subsequently, but it is doubtful whether the previous defect of intelligence is ever made good completely, although the physical appearance may become completely normal.

### 4. *Infantile Hyperuricaemia* (*Lesch–Nyhan Syndrome*)

This condition is inherited in an X-linked manner. There is a deficiency of the enzyme hypoxanthine-guanine phosphoribosyl transferase (HGPRT), as a result of which there is a disturbance of purine metabolism, leading to an accumulation of uric acid in the blood and severe brain damage.

Affected males develop normally until they are a few weeks old, when they give an excessive 'startle' reaction with attacks of hypertonia. Spasticity increases and cerebral palsy and choreo-athetosis develop and mental deterioration is progressive. The appetite is poor, but the thirst is excessive and attacks of haematuria may occur. Death usually occurs before puberty.

A particularly distressing feature of this disorder is the tendency to extreme self-mutilation, which takes the form of chewing their lips away and biting the fingers down to the bone in spite of the obvious pain they cause themselves. While they are doing this, the children seem to be terrified and are obviously relieved when restrained.

The administration of allopurinol reduces the level of uric acid in the blood, but does not prevent or reduce the degree of brain damage, for which there is no known treatment. However, the condition may be detected during pregnancy by enzyme estimations on fibroblast cultures obtained by amniocentesis and termination of pregnancy considered.

## 5. *Nephrogenic Diabetes Insipidus*

This condition is inherited in an X-linked manner and, except in rare cases, affects only males. The exact nature of the metabolic disorder is not known, but there is a complete failure of the kidney tubules to respond to the posterior pituitary hormone, pitressin. As a result, there is a failure of control of the passage of water from the blood to the kidneys. Soon after birth the child passes large volumes of urine, develops an excessive thirst, vomits, becomes dehydrated and has frequent convulsions and may run erratic fevers.

This condition, which persists throughout life, causes mental subnormality unless the dehydration is prevented by a continuous large water intake. Fluid loss may be considerably reduced by administering ethacrynic acid with potassium chloride supplements.

Carriers may be detected by urine concentration tests on women in whom the condition is suspected.

ICHTHYOSIS

Ichthyosis (scaliness of the skin) is a feature of the following three conditions associated with mental subnormality, which may be due to inborn errors of metabolism:

1. *Rud's Syndrome*. This is inherited in an autosomal recessive manner. Mental subnormality, ichthyosis, dwarfism, infantilism, epilepsy, polyneuritis and anaemia are present.

55

2. *X-linked Ichthyosis*. Mental subnormality, ichthyosis and hypogonadism are present in males only, except in very rare cases.

3. *Sjögren–Larsson Syndrome*. This is inherited in an autosomal recessive manner. Mental subnormality, ichthyosis, macular degeneration of the retina and spastic paraplegia are present and convulsions may occur. Sweating is absent except on the face and the backs of the hands.

## CASES OF AMENTIA WITHOUT KNOWN GENETIC CAUSES

A number of cases of amentia are attributable more directly to environmental than to genetic causes. These causes may operate during either pregnancy or labour or subsequently at any time before the genetically determined limits of intelligence have been reached. They include anything which can interfere with the nutrition or oxygenation of the brain or may destroy previously normal brain cells.

The growth of the brain does not proceed at an even rate throughout intra-uterine life, but takes place in two spurts of activity. During the first, which occurs between the 15th and 20th week of gestation, the neurons are multiplying to reach their adult number, and during the second, which starts at the 25th week and continues until the second year of postnatal life, glial cell multiplication is taking place. The weight of the developing brain is directly correlated with the general body weight of the fetus at that time, and nutritional deficiencies at the time of either brain growth spurt may produce deficiences of brain growth and intelligence which can never be made up subsequently by adequate nutrition. Premature babies who are light for their gestational age are more likely to be mentally subnormal than those premature babies of normal weight for their gestational age. Full-term babies, too, who are light for their gestational age, run a higher risk of being mentally subnormal than those of normal birth weight.

## A. NUTRITIONAL AMENTIA

From what has been said it will be clear that any nutritional deficiency, such as protein lack, which can cause retardation of general body growth may result in intellectual deficiency if it occurs at the time of the brain growth spurt. During intra-uterine life, placental insufficiency is an important cause of poor fetal growth. Placental insufficiency may be due to developmental abnormalities of the placenta or various maternal disorders, such as cardiovascular disease, repeated antenatal haemorrhages, chronic renal disease, toxaemia of pregnancy or severe diabetes mellitus. In the latter, fetal hypoglycaemia, induced by treatment of the maternal diabetes, may be an additional adverse influence on fetal development. Smoking during pregnancy causes fetal underdevelopment, partly by causing vasoconstriction and reduced placental blood flow and hypoxia, and partly by depleting the maternal stores of vitamin $B_{12}$, upon which the fetus makes heavy demands for its normal development.

There is a greater risk of underdevelopment in multiple than in single pregnancies.

Low maternal urinary oestriol excretion is an important indication of retarded fetal growth. Early recognition of retarded fetal growth and, if possible, the treatment of its cause or the correction of postnatal dietary deficiencies before the period of brain growth spurt ends, may avoid any impairment of intelligence.


## 1. *NEONATAL HYPOGLYCAEMIA*

Babies who are light for their gestational age are particularly likely to develop hypoglycaemia, due to their poor stores of glycogen in the liver. Where the blood glucose level is allowed to remain below 20 mg/100 ml death may occur, or permanent brain damage and mental subnormality may result. The signs of neonatal hypoglycaemia include a poor sucking reflex, apnoeic attacks, convulsions, restlessness and abnormal sensitivity to auditory and tactile stimuli, to which the baby responds with widespread tremors.

To reduce the risk of permanent brain damage, the acute symptoms are treated by intravenous transfusion of glucose, perhaps with hydrocortisone injections, until the blood glucose level has remained above 20 mg/100 ml for 12 hours.


## 2. *ANOXIA*

The human brain is capable of surviving deprivation of oxygen for only very short periods and the brain of the fetus is very sensitive to anoxia. Anoxia may arise during pregnancy, due to placental insufficiency associated with developmental abnormalities, preeclamptic toxaemia or retroplacental haemorrhage. It may arise at birth, due to interference with the circulation by a prolonged second stage of labour or prolapse of the umbilical cord. Neonatal anoxia may be the result of depression of the baby's respiratory centre by heavy maternal sedation. Babies of low birth weight for their gestational age are particularly prone to the effects of anoxia and are likely also to be hypoglycaemic, due to their heavy demand on liver glycogen stores. Any severe respiratory infection in early childhood, before the brain growth spurt is complete, may cause anoxic brain damage.

## B. AMENTIA DUE TO INFECTION

### 1. *MATERNAL INFECTIONS*

#### a. Due to Viruses

The seare most likely to interfere with development of the fetus when they occur during the first 3 months of pregnancy, as in the case of rubella.

#### i. *Rubella (German measles)*

The risk has been estimated as 60 per cent if the mother contracts rubella 3–4 weeks after the onset of her last menstrual period, as 35 per cent at 5–8 weeks, as 15 per cent at 9–12 weeks and as 7 per cent at 13–16 weeks, with an overall risk up to 16 weeks of 21 per cent. Maternal rubella without a rash or subclinical maternal rubella can also cause serious fetal damage. Subclinical infection is more likely in women who are reinfected after a vaccine-induced immunity than in those with a disease-induced immunity.

Affected children are usually microcephalic, with abnormalities of the eyes such as microphthalmia, cataracts, glaucoma or retinitis pigmentosa, and they may be deaf and have congenital heart defects. Their growth is frequently retarded, and shortly after birth they may suffer from thrombocytopenic purpura and hepatitis, both of which usually resolve spontaneously. The degree of mental subnormality varies, from severe, in the case of early maternal infections, to mild, in the case of later infections. It may be associated with speech disorders or autistic behaviour.

Dermatoglyphics show a significantly increased incidence of whorl patterns on the finger-tips and of simian creases or the so-called 'Sydney line' (which is formed by the extension of the proximal transverse palmar crease to the ulnar border of the hand). The risk of serious fetal complications of maternal rubella may be considered sufficient to justify termination of pregnancy, if the mother wishes this. It is hoped to reduce the incidence of congenital rubella by vaccinating adolescent schoolgirls and non-pregnant women who lack rubella antibodies with attenuated living viruses.

Although most attention has been focused on maternal rubella, evidence is accumulating of the possible importance of other virus infections during the first 3-months of pregnancy as causes of mental subnormality, although they cause less severe congenital abnormalities. These include infections with cytomegalovirus, varicella (chicken pox), herpes simplex, infectious heptatitis, influenza A virus, mumps virus and poliomyelitis virus.

## ii. *Cytomegalovirus Infection*

Evidence is accumulating that maternal cytomegalovirus infection may be responsible for far more cases of amentia in the offspring than maternal rubella.

As in the case of rubella, the fetus is more likely to be affected when maternal infection occurs early in pregnancy, but, in contrast to maternal rubella, the fetus may be infected late in pregnancy and the overall risk of 50 per cent is higher than in the case of rubella. The maternal infection is usually subclinical and unrecognized.

Affected children are born prematurely, with breathing difficulties, jaundice, hepatosplenomegaly and thrombocytopenic purpura. Many die within a few days of birth. Those that survive are usually microcephalic, with chorioretinitis, and may later develop infantile spasms or epilepsy and cerebral palsy and show varying degrees of mental subnormality.

Dermatoglyphics: as in the case of congenital rubella there is an increased frequency of whorl patterns on the finger tips and of Sydney lines on the palms.

## iii. *Varicella* (*chicken pox*)

Congenital abnormalities which have been reported after maternal varicella during the first trimester of pregnancy include limb deformities and the presence of skin scars along the length of the hypoplastic limb. The birth weight may be low and there may be feeding difficulties and failure to thrive, and chorioretinitis may be present and meningoencephalitis may occur. As a result of the latter there may be brain damage and mental subnormality.

## b. Due to Other Organisms

### i. *Syphilis*

This is fortunately a rare cause of amentia nowadays, but may take two main forms in the child:

CONGENITAL SYPHILIS

In this condition both mental and physical development may be obviously affected from birth, but usually the latter more than the former. The affected infant is anaemic and fails to thrive and may have a maculopapular skin rash. All organs of the body may be affected. Growth is stunted and the facial appearance is typical, with the so-called 'saddle-back' deformity of the nose, due to defective development of the bridge. Abnormalities of dentition occur, of which the most typical gives the upper central incisors a peg-shaped appearance, with a crescentic notch of the biting edge (Hutchinson's teeth). There are frequently developmental abnormalities of the eyes, including opacities of the cornea, strabismus and nystagmus. The central nervous system is affected to a variable degree and epilepsy may occur. The Wassermann reaction is not sufficiently constant in these cases for any diagnostic reliance to be placed on it.

JUVENILE TABOPARESIS

In this condition mental development may be normal until the age of about 9 or 10 years, when signs of adult taboparesis occur, with the characteristic disturbances of co-ordination and gait and spastic paralysis of the limbs. The reflex changes vary according to the relative involvement of the motor or sensory systems. Dementia occurs at first slowly, but progresses rapidly in the terminal stages and is accompanied by frequent epileptic fits. Death usually occurs within 10 years from the appearance of the first signs.

It may be possible to avert the progress of the disease with antibiotics, but the probabilities of normal mental development subsequently are extremely remote.

Positive Wassermann reactions in blood and cerebrospinal fluid occur more frequently than in congenital syphilis, and other characteristic changes occur in the cerebrospinal fluid, which gives a Lange gold curve of typical pattern.

## ii. *Toxoplasmosis*

This is an infection by the protozoa *Toxoplasma gondii*, which is acquired from farm and domestic animals and which usually causes only mild symptoms in adult humans.

Serological evidence of infection at some time has been found in as many as 50 per cent of pregnant women in some country districts, but it is necessary for the primary infection of the mother to occur during pregnancy for the infection to be transmitted to the fetus. Transmission can occur throughout pregnancy, but the earlier the maternal infection the greater is the probability of fetal death and abortion. Where transmission occurs during the second half of pregnancy, the fetus may survive to term and show evidence of congenital infection at birth or this may not become apparent until the infant is several weeks old. The infection causes a severe encephalomyelitis, as a result of which either microcephaly or a mild hydrocephalus may occur, associated with various spastic deformities, convulsions and bilateral choroidoretinitis. Unilateral

microphthalmia may occur. The liver and spleen are enl
Calcification of the scattered areas of brain damage may be ap
in radiographs.

The degree of mental subnormality will vary according
severity of the brain damage.

The diagnosis can be confirmed by various serological tests.

## 2. CHILDHOOD INFECTIONS

### a. Due to Viruses

*Encephalitis*

This may arise as a primary infection of the brain or as a rare complication of any of the common virus infections of children. In the
latter case its occurrence is often unrelated to the severity of the
primary infection or to the effects on the fetus of maternal infection
with the same virus. In some cases recovery may be complete. In
other cases there may be signs of residual brain damage: hemiplegia,
ataxia, aphasia, choreiform or athetoid movements, convulsions and
varying degrees of mental subnormality. The effect on intelligence
may be relatively slight compared with the great disturbance of
behaviour and personality which may result. This may take the form
of pathological lying, stealing, viciousness and sexual behaviour.

Acute encephalitis lethargica, which rarely occurs as a major
epidemic, but which may occur sporadically at any time, may cause
amentia.

In amentia due to encephalitis lethargica, as in that due to meningitis, the impairment of intelligence may be less marked than the
resulting personality change. However, encephalitis lethargica may
damage the ganglia at the base of the brain sufficiently to produce
post-encephalitic Parkinsonism, sometimes after an interval of years.
The main signs of this condition are a generalized slowing of the
bodily movements due to increased muscular rigidity, which gives a
characteristic 'cog-wheel' sensation on passive movement of the
joints. The normal mobility of the facial expression becomes lost and
excessive salivation may occur. There may be periodic painful involuntary spasms of the external muscles of the eyes, as a result of
which they become turned upwards so that only the whites are
visible ('oculogyric crises'). The associated movements of the arms
and legs in walking are lost and there may be a pill-rolling tremor
of the thumb and first finger. In some cases hemiparesis occurs.

There is no specific treatment, but drugs are available to reduce
the muscular rigidity and excessive salivation. Attempts are being
made to treat the symptoms by localized brain operations.

The patient's slowness of response and movement should not be
taken as a measure of his intellectual capacity and it should never

be forgotten that in many cases the patient's understanding of events around him is not grossly impaired. For this reason the greatest care should always be taken to avoid statements in his presence which might be hurtful or embarrassing to him.

A clear-cut history of preceding encephalitis is frequently absent in patients developing signs of post-encephalitic Parkinsonism, but the abnormal sensitivity of a number of cases of amentia to the extra-pyramidal effects of various tranquillizing drugs suggests the possibility that their amentia may, in fact, be due to undiagnosed encephalitis.

On fortunately very rare occasions, severe brain damage and mental subnormality may occur as a result of a post-vaccination encephalitis arising after vaccination against one of the virus diseases of childhood or against whooping cough.

### b. Due to other Organisms

*Meningitis*

This may occur in an acute form in primary cerebrospinal meningitis or as a complication of generalized bacterial infections or in a chronic form in tuberculous meningitis. In each case, the underlying cortex may be damaged with resulting neurological abnormalities and mental subnormality, or mainly a personality change, as in some cases of encephalitis as mentioned above.

In some cases of meningitis, adhesions develop at the base of the brain which interfere with the circulation of cerebrospinal fluid and produce hydrocephalus, as a result of which the skull may be grossly enlarged in the characteristically globular fashion. There may be defects of vision and hearing and other signs of involvement of the central nervous system, depending upon the severity of the hydro-cephalus.

The course of hydrocephalus is variable: it may progress rapidly to death in a short period or may develop slowly for a period until a balance between secretion and absorption of cerebrospinal fluid becomes established. During the stage of active development the fontanelles remain open and epileptic fits occur, but often cease later.

In all severe cases of hydrocephalus, cerebral atrophy occurs and there are severe amentia and wasting of the body, with spasticity of upper and lower limbs and eventual development of contractures. The patients are very prone to develop bed sores and, due to decalcification of their bones, spontaneous fractures frequently occur. The great weight of the head predisposes them to dislocation of the neck if unsupported during carrying. Death normally occurs owing to intercurrent infection of the chest or urinary tracts.

Attempts to find a drug to control the secretion of cerebrospinal fluid have so far proved unsuccessful, but it is possible to by-pass the site of the obstruction to the circulation of cerebrospinal fluid by providing a shunt between the ventricular and vascular systems, by means of a Spitz–Holter or Pudenz valve, which allows a constant small volume of fluid to pass. If the flow is adjusted so that the ventricle is allowed to increase in size very slowly, the ependymal surface may become sufficient to absorb the net amount of fluid which cannot be absorbed through the normal channels. Unfortunately, the shunt systems are very prone to become infected and obstructed and have to be replaced periodically.

In childhood, any illness which produces dehydration, such as severe gastro-intestinal infection, may cause hypernatraemia and brain damage. In some of these cases, thrombosis of the venous sinuses draining the brain may occur and result in paralysis of the opposite side of the body, epilepsy and severe amentia. Severe brain damage and amentia may sometimes follow hyperpyrexia accompanying relatively trivial childhood infections such as tonsillitis or otitis media.

## C. AMENTIA DUE TO TRAUMA

Direct violence during pregnancy is rarely a cause of amentia. A sufficient degree of violence to the mother to affect the fetus directly is more likely to cause a stillbirth. There are, however, various other physical influences to which the mother may be subjected which may prove sufficiently harmful to the developing fetus to result in amentia.

### i. *Excessive Exposure to Radiation*

This may cause brain damage during the first trimester, whether it is the result of diagnostic X-ray examination of the lower abdomen or of atomic radiation, as in Hiroshima, where all 8 women survivors who were within 1200 m of the atomic explosion and who were between the 7th and 15th week of pregnancy at the time gave birth to microcephalic children. Other survivors have been found to have abnormal chromosomes which persist to this day. Exposure to excessive radiation may also produce mutation of genes, usually of recessive type, which may increase the probability that the members of subsequent generations may suffer from amentia. Present evidence suggests that the use of diagnostic ultrasound during pregnancy carries with it a far smaller risk of causing fetal abnormalities than diagnostic X-ray at that time.

## ii. *Teratogenic Substances*

It is possible that substances used unsuccessfully to prevent conception or to induce abortion may yet damage the fertilized ovum sufficiently to cause congenital abnormalities and amentia in the offspring. There is, however, no definite evidence that either may be caused by hormonal pregnancy tests.

### α. CAMPTOMELIC DWARFISM (SYNDROME OF MULTIPLE OSSEOUS DEFORMITIES)

In this syndrome the following congenital abnormalities are present: flat face, hypertelorism, micrognathia (small mouth), cleft palate and low-set ears. The scapulae, clavicles and ribs are hypoplastic. There is anterior bowing of the femora and tibiae, with a cutaneous dimple over the point of maximal deformity. The fibulae are hypoplastic and there is a talipes equinovarus deformity of the feet. A bilateral Sydney line may be present on the palms.

It is suggested that camptomelic dwarfism is caused by folic acid antagonists such as aminopterin or methotrexate, which are both used in the treatment of psoriasis and have a reputation as abortifacients.

Where the fully developed syndrome is present, the baby suffers from severe respiratory distress and dies in early infancy. Less severely affected babies may survive and are likely to be mentally subnormal.

Somewhat similar, but less severe, congenital abnormalities have been reported in the offspring of epileptic women taking anticonvulsants of the barbiturate and hydantoinate groups, both of which are known folic acid antagonists, during pregnancy. Affected children may be microcephalic, with hypertelorism, low-set ears, hare-lip and cleft palate, a short neck with a low posterior hairline and cardiac and minor skeletal abnormalities. A bilateral simian crease may be present, and mental subnormality of varying degrees of severity.

Folic acid dietary supplements throughout pregnancy may reduce the incidence of these abnormalities.

Craniofacial malformations and abnormalities of the central nervous system have also been reported in the offspring of mothers who took tricyclic antidepressants during the first trimester of pregnancy.

### β. ANENCEPHALY

In the complete form of anencephaly the brain may be entirely absent at birth, or absent except for the cerebellum and part of the basal ganglia, and is often associated with spina bifida. The condition is incompatible with survival. It is, therefore, not itself a significant cause of mental subnormality, but it may be associated with other developmental abnormalities of the brain, possibly of related aetiology, occurring in later siblings. The cause of anencephaly is not known, but an increased incidence has been reported following epidemics of potato blight and it has been claimed that affected potatoes contain a substance which is teratogenic if ingested during pregnancy. These claims are, as yet, unproved and there is some evidence to suggest a genetic factor in that immigrants carry with them the incidence of their mother country.

Anencephaly may be diagnosed during pregnancy by ultrasound or by detecting abnormally high levels of $\alpha$-fetoprotein in the amniotic fluid.

γ. RHESUS FACTOR INCOMPATIBILITY

The offspring of a woman with Rhesus-negative (Rh-negative) blood and a man with Rhesus-positive (Rh-positive) blood will have Rhesus-positive blood. The brain of the offspring may be damaged sufficiently to cause amentia as a result of the incompatibility between the mother's and the baby's blood. The mother starts to become immunised and to develop antibodies to the baby's blood during the first pregnancy, whether this continues to term or ends in either spontaneous or therapeutic abortion after the end of the first trimester. The child of the first conception is not usually affected, but later children are likely to be jaundiced at birth and subsequently to develop rigidity and athetosis due to damage to the basal ganglia by bile pigment ('kernicterus').

The development of antibodies and subsequent fetal damage may be prevented by injecting non-immunized Rhesus-negative women with anti-D γ-globulin within 48 hours of delivery. Where maternal immunization has already occurred and amniocentesis indicates a rising concentration of bilirubin due to destruction of fetal red blood cells, fetal damage may be reduced or prevented by injecting packed red blood cells into the fetal peritoneal cavity *in utero* or carrying out a complete exchange transfusion on the fetal blood *in utero*. Exchange transfusions may also be carried out immediately after birth if the condition has not previously been diagnosed. The necessity for exchange transfusions may be reduced by giving phenobarbitone to mothers during the last 2 weeks of pregnancy. It has been claimed that phototherapy of affected infants also reduces this necessity. Phenobarbitone and phototherapy may be effective also in reducing hyperbilirubinaemia and the risk of brain damage in premature or 'light-for-dates' babies or due to drugs such as long-acting sulphonamides taken late in pregnancy.

It has been suggested that Rhesus factor incompatibility may cause damage *in utero* and amentia, even when there is no motor involvement history of jaundice at birth, and it has been reported that the idence of Rhesus-negative blood is twice as high in the mothers the mentally subnormal as in mothers of normal children.

### iii. *Precipitate Labour*

When the second stage of labour is too rapid for proper moulding of the baby's head to take place, the brain may be damaged either directly or as the result of haemorrhage due to the tearing of the cerebral blood vessels. The damage is usually unilateral, with hemiplegia on the opposite side of the body and a high incidence of epilepsy and varying degrees of amentia. In some cases, hydrocephalus may result from obstruction to the circulation of cerebrospinal fluid by adhesions following haemorrhage at the base of the brain. The condition has to be distinguished from congenital dysplegia of intra-uterine origin, which is the result of excessive exposure to radiation, intra-uterine infections, anoxia or nutritional defects. In these cases there is often a history of an easy birth of normal duration, with symmetrical spastic paralysis, athetosis or chorea and amentia, but with epilepsy an uncommon sequel.

### iv. *Cerebral Trauma in Childhood*

Among the most tragic cases of amentia are those following accidental external violence to the skull in children of previously normal intelligence. The brain may also be damaged by multiple capillary haemorrhages which sometimes occur as a result of increased intracranial pressure during severe and prolonged bouts of coughing in whooping cough.

## D. AMENTIA DUE TO POISONOUS SUBSTANCES

The developing brain may also be damaged by the ingestion of various poisonous metallic substances such as lead, copper, manganese and strontium. Lead poisoning occurs most frequently between the ages of 18 months and 3 years in children who live in poor urban areas and suck or chew lead-containing paints crumbling from the walls of old houses. It may also arise from the inhalation of lead dust. In the most serious cases, lead encephalopathy occurs with blindness, deafness, convulsions and severe amentia. In less severe cases, affected children tend to be withdrawn, irritable and disobedient and to show some autistic features or periodic psychotic behaviour. They may develop polyneuritis and optic atrophy. In all cases, the level of lead in the blood is increased and anaemia occurs with abnormalities in both red and white cells. Lead lines may be seen in X-rays of the bones.

The degree of brain damage may be reduced by facilitating the excretion of lead from the body in a non-toxic form by giving calcium versenate intravenously to severe cases or D-penicillamine orally to milder cases in older children and adults.

It is possible that mental subnormality may result from brain damage due to methaemoglobinaemia caused by the ingestion of spinach with a high nitrite content due to incorrect preparation.

## E. ISOLATION AMENTIA

The mind requires an external stimulus for its proper development, as do the muscles and bones, and it normally obtains this through the sense organs. If any of these organs are defective in their functioning, disturbance of perception, upon which all higher thought processes are built, is inevitable and in extreme cases, if this is not recognized and appropriate treatment and training given, various degrees of amentia may result. Hence the vital necessity of adequate physical examination of all cases of suspected mental subnormality as early as possible to exclude the presence of any sensory defect such as high frequency deafness, which may interfere with the normal development of speech and masquerade as mental subnormality. However, there is evidence that even when no sensory defect exists, enforced isolation for prolonged periods, during the period of normal development, may produce amentia, as in the case of Kasper Hauser, who, it is claimed, was kept in isolation in a small dark cell for the first 16 years of his life.

## F. PARENTAL REJECTION

It is sometimes suggested that parental rejection is a primary cause of mental subnormality. In the author's view, where rejection occurs, it is, in the vast majority of cases, a secondary result rather than a primary cause and develops out of the parents' frustration and disappointment at their inability to make a satisfactory relationship with the child due to its inherent subnormality. Such parents frequently have a great sense of guilt and to add to it by suggesting they are primarily responsible for their child's condition is unforgivable.

# The Abilities and Behaviour of the Mentally Subnormal

THE existence of the most severely subnormal patient is merely vegetative. The patient is mute, completely helpless and lies in his cot showing no awareness of his surroundings, doubly incontinent, and throughout his life requires the same nursing attention as a small baby. With diminishing degrees of mental subnormality, there is a progressive increase in spontaneous activity, which may include the ingestion of all manner of inedible objects ('pica') as well as the ability for self-care and the control of natural functions. A few words of speech emerge, but the grasp and understanding are very poor; at a lesser degree of mental subnormality there is the ability to answer simple questions and obey simple commands, but not to initiate or maintain a conversation. In the middle range of severe subnormality the latter ability is present, but the patient's thought processes are limited to the perceptual level, with no ability for conceptual thought and with marked defect of reasoning power. These patients are capable of simple routine work under close supervision, but left to themselves show little initiative or planning ability. They have poor powers of concentration. Some can read words of up to four or five letters and can write a letter from a copy, but cannot compose one unaided. Their general knowledge is often limited to that of their immediate surroundings and often they cannot give accurate information about their age, birthday or the present date, and cannot tell the time. They can count in a purely mechanical manner and, although they have have some idea of relative money values, they cannot handle sums larger than about 20 to 30 pence.

At the upper limit of severe subnormality patients can give personal information, know the date, tell the time and can often read quite fluently, but with very little grasp and understanding of the subject matter. They are able to compose and write their own stereotyped letters. The range of general knowledge is superficially good, but obviously defective on questioning. They are capable of such simple concepts as beauty and truth, although they may not always appear to be aware of the latter! They can do additions and subtractions, but fail on problems involving simple reasoning. They are, however, very easily led, and for this reason liable to be exploited either sexually or by unscrupulous employers or to be led into antisocial behaviour by undesirable acquaintances. It is these limitations which render them incapable of leading an independent existence.

The subnormal are closely linked with the problem family group (the so-called 'submerged 10 per cent'), and with Lewis's subcultural group. These patients tend to breed true and to produce children with similar or lesser degrees of intellectual defect, whereas the severely subnormal are more frequently born to parents of average or superior intelligence.

Although of normal appearance, and not grossly defective in ordinary school attainments, the subnormal show no grasp of the principles which govern human behaviour. This is largely the result of their unstable background, in which parental immaturity and inconsistency in admonitions and punishments create confusion and insecurity in the child's mind which its own limitations of intelligence preclude it from resolving. It is not surprising, therefore, that it may rebel against the relative regimentation of school and tasks which it finds difficult, by truancy, seeking bad company and resorting to delinquency. Such individuals are hopelessly inadequate in a modern urban civilization and a number drift into crime and become repeated offenders: drunkenness, larceny, prostitution, neglect of children, indecent assaults, common assaults, arson, suicide and homicide, in that order of frequency.

It is possible to classify this group of individuals in the 'psychopathic disorder' category of the Mental Health Act, 1959, and to call them 'subnormal psychopaths'. The author believes, however, that this practice is unhelpful to the mentally subnormal and is better avoided and that the term 'psychopath' should be confined to individuals whose behaviour disorders are not accompanied by subnormality of intelligence.

The subnormal girl, so often deprived of affection in childhood, is apt to mistake sexual advances from the opposite sex for true affection, so that the incidence of illegitimate births in this group is high.

As might be expected, homosexual behaviour is apt to occur amongst subnormal and severely subnormal patients of both sexes as in any other community, but is less likely where mixing of the sexes is encouraged.

Subnormal patients react badly to admission to hospital if brought into contact with the more severely subnormal whom they sometimes exploit. The two groups of patients should therefore be treated in parts of the hospital remote from each other. The behaviour difficulties of the subnormal patients are potentiated by their collection together in large groups, and it is desirable that they should be treated in wards for not more than 10–15 patients, staffed by most highly selected nurses with a proper understanding of the psychogenesis of their behaviour disorders. The success of such a ward, run as far as possible on permissive and psychotherapeutic lines, depends ultimately on the atmosphere of security, understanding and affection created by the nursing staff who, with the psychiatric staff, must inevitably act as parent substitutes towards the patients. It is, therefore, desirable that the same nursing staff should always work in the ward, as experience has shown that difficulties most frequently develop during the periods when patients are in the care of relief staff with whom they are unfamiliar.

The next stage in the rehabilitation of these patients presents a problem so far not satisfactorily resolved. Their need is for a stable home environment outside of hospital, but few have homes of their own to which they could be discharged with confidence. Neither local health authority hostels nor the majority of available lodgings are adequate substitutes for a real home, and, unfortunately, their choice of marriage partners is often unlikely to provide the stability they need.

Whatever the grade of subnormality, a search should always be made for the cause of any misbehaviour. Even at the lowest level a simple cause will usually be found for a temper outburst in the behaviour of those in immediate contact with the patient. More severe temper outbursts may follow an epileptic fit or represent an epileptic equivalent or may be a manifestation of a psychotic illness. In higher grades it may be related to anxiety about relatives in the absence of letters or visits, jealousy of other patients or resentment of staff attitudes, or may be associated with premenstrual tension. A frequent cause of misbehaviour is a broken promise made to a patient by a relative or member of the staff. No definite promise should ever be made to a mentally subnormal person unless there is a reasonable prospect of its fulfilment. It is important that all staff should recognize these disturbances for what they are and should play their part in alleviating them rather than regarding them merely as aggravations and provocations to be endured and to be explained away simply as the sort of behaviour to be expected of the subnormal, without any specific cause for them.

Serious premeditated planned violence is rare in the mentally subnormal and is likely to occur only in the least handicapped. When violence occurs in more severely subnormal patients, it is usually an immediate response to provocation, similar to the reaction of a normal child of similar mental age, who has not yet learnt self-control.

However, in some severely subnormal patients, impulsive, destructive and aggressive behaviour occurs periodically and quite unpredictably, without any environmental cause. The management of these patients has been revolutionized in recent years by the use of first chlorpromazine and then other phenothiazine derivative drugs and drugs such as haloperidol. Under the control of these drugs many patients become much more manageable and accessible to environmental influences, with great improvement in their behaviour and in the capacity for useful occupation. Since their introduction the necessity for seclusion or restraint has become less frequent, and life for patients and staff has become much more tolerable.

## Hyperkinetic Syndrome

This syndrome, which occurs in childhood, in boys more often than girls, is the result of brain damage due to a number of different causes. Its onset is at any time between a month and 3 years (average 18 months) after the damage.

The cardinal sign of this syndrome is, as the name implies, excessive motor activity. The child is never at rest, often by night as well as by day. Its activity is not directed to any useful purpose and often takes the form of destructiveness and viciousness towards other children. The child's concentration is very poor, the child is easily distracted and there is no ability for sustained affection. The mood fluctuates against a background of euphoria and the child shows a lack of shyness and fear.

In addition to mental subnormality—usually severe—there are epileptic fits and EEG abnormalities, often of spike and wave type. The overactivity is aggravated by barbiturates and the fits are best controlled with hydantoinates and primidone. Paradoxically, in some cases, overactivity is reduced by treatment with amphetamine, possibly due to its stimulation of cortical controlling centres.

When the brain damage is less severe, the child's general overactivity may be less obvious. However, he is characteristically awkward and excessively clumsy when tying his shoes, catching a ball or learning to ride a bicycle. He may show motor impersistence and be unable to maintain voluntary movements, such as keeping his eyes closed, fixing his gaze in a lateral direction, keeping his mouth open, or protruding his tongue.

The brain-damaged child may also have disorders of perception, such as disturbance of spatial relationships, concept of body-image and right–left orientation.

71

# Epilepsy in
# the Mentally Subnormal

CONVULSIONS in newborn babies may be due either to metabolic disorders or to brain damage. The latter, which tend to occur in the first 3 days of life or after the eighth day, have a worse prognosis than the former, which tend to occur between the fifth and the eighth day. Of particularly serious prognosis as regards progressive mental deterioration, dementia and severe degrees of mental subnormality are the 'infantile spasms' (or 'salaam' spasms) in the first year of life, in which the child suddenly falls forwards and prostrates itself in the prone position. Such attacks are associated with a characteristic pattern in the EEG called 'hypsarrhythmia', but this EEG abnormality may be present with a similarly serious prognosis without the presence of salaam spasms. Hypsarrhythmia may result from a variety of causes of brain damage, including hypersensitivity to immunization in infancy against various diseases. The hypsarrhythmic pattern may be abolished by the administration of cortisone, but the prognosis as regards normal mental development remains bad, being relatively better when infantile spasms are absent initially.

In the so-called 'Lennox syndrome', there is progressive mental deterioration, starting between the ages of 1 and 6 years. Two types of seizure occur: one similar to petit mal and the other, in which a sudden tonic, but never clonic, seizure affects the limbs. The EEG abnormalities are distinctive from those in hypsarrhythmia and true petit mal. The seizures in Lennox syndrome do not respond to the usual drugs used in the treatment of grand mal and petit mal, but they are said to respond to diazepam.

Epilepsy is a frequent accompaniment of mental subnormality, particularly of the more severe degree in older patients. Major (grand mal) and minor (petit mal) fits may occur in the same patient, and the former may be immediately preceded by periods of unstable behaviour, which may still occur even if the fit itself is prevented by anticonvulsant drugs. Particularly is this true at the time of menstruation. In other patients showing periodic unstable behaviour, there may never have been any typical fits, but its epileptic basis is revealed by characteristic patterns in the EEG record. This is particularly true where the EEG reveals a focus of disturbed function in the temporal lobe—so-called 'temporal lobe epilepsy'. In such cases, marked improvement in behaviour, without any appreciable disturbance of mental capacity, may follow removal of the part of the temporal lobe containing the epileptic focus. Some cases of apparent grand mal or petit mal seizures which are resistant to the usual drug treatments of these conditions may, in fact, be cases of temporal lobe epilepsy and require treatment with the drugs which are specific for that condition.

Myoclonic epilepsy, in which involuntary jerking of a limb without loss of consciousness is a manifestation of cerebral dysrhythmia, is a fairly common accompaniment of those cases of severe subnormality due to encephalitis or meningitis.

Other types of epilepsy are uncommon in the mentally subnormal.

# Mental Illness in
# the Mentally Subnormal

ALL forms of mental illness—psychosis, neurosis and organic reaction types—may occur in the mentally subnormal, but their relative frequency varies with different degrees of mental subnormality, although when a case is first seen after dementia has occurred, it may be difficult to assess accurately the pre-psychotic intellectual level. Because of the poor personality integration in many of the mentally subnormal, mental illness occurs among them more commonly in mixed than in classic textbook forms.

## A. PSYCHOSES

1. True, alternating manic-depressive psychosis occurs most frequently when the degree of mental subnormality is least, but the particular types of psychotic depression, which occur at specific periods such as the menopause or during the involutional period, occur also in patients at the upper end of the range of severe subnormality, including those with Down's syndrome, and mild chronic mania also is not uncommon in this group.

2. Schizophrenia occurs through a wider range of mental subnormality than the manic-depressive psychosis, but when its onset is in childhood (juvenile schizophrenia), it may arrest mental development and thus, itself, be a cause of mental subnormality. In juvenile schizophrenia there is a history of normal early development preceding progressive disintegration of personality, and it seems probable that it is due to a genetically determined biochemical disorder.

When subjected to stress, the mentally subnormal, including those with Down's syndrome, sometimes develop disorders of perception and of their sense of reality to the extent of becoming deluded and hallucinated. These episodes, which usually respond well to treatment with phenothiazines and psychotherapy, are best referred to as 'schizoid reactions' to distinguish them from true schizophrenia, with its much more serious prognosis.

## B. PSEUDO-PSYCHOSES

It is not uncommon for the mentally subnormal to describe in some detail, and with considerable conviction, events which have no basis in fact. In some cases, the fantasies are of a harmless nature and are akin to those of small children, and in others, apparent delusions, as of pregnancy, are obvious attention-seeking devices.

In some cases, such as those in which sexual interference by another person is alleged, this appears to be a wish-fulfilment fantasy when that person is an unattainable love-object or, conversely, an attempt to harm a person disliked by the patient. Such allegations are very distressing to the innocent victims of patients' attentions, but it is sometimes extremely difficult to establish their innocence in the face of patients' insistence on the truth of their statements and the absence of supporting or refuting evidence. Where such allegations concern an employer and are shown or admitted by the patient to be untrue, the possibility of the patient's future employment outside hospital may be prejudiced.

The sex chromosome abnormalities associated with mental subnormality in both males and females are associated also with an increased liability to develop psychotic disorders.

## C. NEUROSES

Although an acute anxiety state may appear in both subnormal and severely subnormal patients as an immediate response to a temporarily threatening situation, a chronic anxiety state, due to an unresolved conflict, is confined to the subnormal and those at the upper end of the severely subnormal range. Similarly, reactive depressions are usually less severe and of shorter duration in the severely subnormal than in those of higher intelligence.

Obsessional ruminations may appear secondarily in anxiety states and disappear when the underlying condition is resolved, but true obsessional-compulsive neurosis is a rare occurrence in mental subnormality of any degree.

Conversion hysteria is not uncommon.

## D. ORGANIC REACTION TYPES

As might be expected, the effects of any organic cerebral disease are more marked in the mentally subnormal than in the normal population. Thus, normal senile mental changes appear much earlier and progress more rapidly in the mentally subnormal, particularly in those with Down's syndrome.

Where congenital syphilitic infection has occurred, mental development may be arrested in childhood and be followed by the rapid dementia of juvenile general paralysis of the insane (juvenile GPI).

Acute confusional episodes may accompany intercurrent infections and generally disappear with the infection, but more prolonged confusion and mental slowing may be due to the toxic effect of drugs such as the anticonvulsants, or may be an indication of vitamin $B_{12}$ or folic acid deficiency, which are by no means uncommon in the mentally subnormal receiving anticonvulsants for epilepsy. They may also be due to nicotinic acid deficiency, as part of the clinical picture of pellagra. Epilepsy itself is, of course, a cause of dementia.

## E. INFANTILE AUTISM

Unfortunately, 'autistic' has taken over from 'spastic' as the currently fashionable euphemism to describe any mentally subnormal child who has difficulties of communication, with the false implication that the prognosis of such cases is better than those of mentally subnormal children without these difficulties. Such a non-specific use of the term 'autistic' makes it meaningless for diagnostic purposes and its use should be confined to children showing the following features obvious from birth:

1. Failure to develop normal interpersonal relationships. The autistic baby shows a characteristic disinclination to cuddle and later tends to avoid direct gaze and shows an increasing withdrawal from social contacts, secondary to

2. Difficulty in comprehending spoken and gesture language and in developing normal and gestural speech. This appears to be the primary disability in autism. Some autistic children never learn to speak. In others, the development of speech is delayed and is characteristically echolalic, with immediate repetition of words just heard or constant repetition of words heard in the more remote past. Words tend to be confused with those of similar sounds or to be mispronounced and the sequence of letters in words or of words in sentences to be muddled. Normal intonation is absent.

Autistic children are late in learning to point at objects and do so in a vague, imprecise way. They do not learn to make use of mime or facial gesture themselves in communication or understand its use by others.

3. Rigid patterns of behaviour with strong resistance to change. Autistic children show rigid patterns of behaviour which they carry out with ritualistic fervour, and include abnormal attachment to favourite objects such as a tin lid, a shoelace or cup. Any attempt to alter the pattern of behaviour or to separate an autistic child from his favourite object may produce a violent emotional reaction or outburst of temper. A similar outburst may be precipitated by the presence of a particular everyday object or some rearrangement of objects in their environment from their normal, familiar pattern. In these episodes, an autistic child may become aggressive or may inflict injuries on himself by biting his hands or wrists. When less

excited, the child may carry out various stereotyped movements such as flicking his fingers in front of his eyes, flapping his hands, grimacing, jumping up and down or walking on tip-toes.

In addition to their speech problems, autistic children have difficulties in understanding their visual perceptions, and, as a result, tend to prefer to explore their environment by touching, tasting and smelling objects around them. They may also confuse right and left, up and down and may find it very difficult to copy skilled movements made by others.

Seventy per cent of autistic children have IQs below 70, with IQs below 50 in 40 per cent. It is now believed that autism, which occurs about three times as often in boys as in girls, has an underlying organic neurological pathology, possibly of genetic origin. It has been suggested that autism is associated with neurophysiological dysfunction of the reticular activating system in the brain stem.

There is no specific treatment for autism, but tranquillizers may be useful in reducing overactivity, and claims have been made for the beneficial effects of operant conditioning in helping autistic children to acquire specific skills and to modify their disturbed behaviour. The prognosis is best in children with IQs over 60. However, there is no evidence that for equal expenditure of time and manpower the prognosis in the case of autistic children is better than that of non-autistic subnormal children of similar IQ.

Autism should not be confused with specific developmental dyslexia, in which impaired language development occurs in the form of a specific delay in learning to read and spell, in association with otherwise high general intelligence and stable behaviour. As in autism, the incidence is higher in boys than in girls and there is difficulty in distinguishing left from right, and probably an underlying genetically determined neurological lesion.

# Drugs in the Care of the Mentally Subnormal

THERE are many drugs used in the treatment of general medical conditions which may occur in the mentally subnormal, but which are not specifically associated with mental subnormality. They will be referred to only when their use demands special care in this condition. The main concern of this chapter is with drugs used in the common accompaniments of mental subnormality.

## A. EPILEPSY

Phenobarbitone, phenytoin and primidone are probably the drugs most frequently used in the treatment of grand mal. However, in the mentally subnormal, grand mal commonly complicates temporal lobe epilepsy, in which phenobarbitone and the hydantoinates used in the treatment of grand mal are not effective. The underlying temporal lobe epilepsy requires more specific treatment (such as sulthiame or carbamazepine), as do minor temporal lobe attacks, which are commonly confused with petit mal. In the latter cases, phenobarbitone and specific petit mal treatments, such as ethosuximide, are ineffective.

Status epilepticus in the mentally subnormal has been most frequently treated in the past by intramuscular injections of paraldehyde in doses of 5–10 ml. However, it is being superseded by diazepam given intravenously in 10-mg doses, slowly increased until 40–50 mg have been given over a period of 1–2 hours. In children, the diazepam may be given as a suppository in a dosage of 0·2 mg/kg body weight, which may bring the seizures under control within 20 minutes.

Phenytoin may produce toxic effects, particularly in children, when the plasma level exceeds 35 μg/ml. The most common are cerebellar ataxia and nystagmus, a morbilliform rash and gum hypertrophy, which may require surgical excision by a dental surgeon. High plasma levels of phenytoin are more likely to occur when other drugs such as sulthiame and diazepam are given concurrently.

All anticonvulsant drugs tend to lower the serum folate level, with the risk of producing mental deterioration, but combinations of anticonvulsants are worse than single drugs. Administration of folic acid

78

alone may produce an increase in the frequency of fits and a fall in the serum vitamin $B_{12}$ level, which if untreated may result in subacute combined degeneration of the spinal cord. This does not happen if folic acid and vitamin $B_{12}$ are given together. Doses of folic acid, 5mg once a week, and of vitamin $B_{12}$, 250 μg once a month, are effective in preventing mental deterioration when given as soon as a patient is put on anticonvulsant drugs. The dosage of either may have to be increased in established cases to correct the abnormal serum levels. Yeast tablets at the rate of three a day may prove equally effective in preventing both folate and vitamin $B_{12}$ deficiency at very much less cost.

## B. SPASTICITY

Diazepam, in doses between about 8 and 16 mg a day, is effective in reducing spasticity, but derivatives of γ-amino-butyric acid (GABA) may prove to be even more effective.

## C. BEHAVIOUR DISORDERS

The search continues for drugs to modify disturbed behaviour in the mentally subnormal without affecting their level of consciousness. The barbiturates were widely used in the past but may, in fact, increase hyperactivity, particularly in brain-damaged children and may cause further mental deterioration. Nowadays, the drugs most frequently used are the tranquillizers and claims have been made for the specific effectiveness of the majority of them in individual cases. In choosing a tranquilliser it may be helpful to bear the following points in mind.

### 1. *PHENOTHIAZINES*

#### a. Dimethyl-aminopropyl Side-chain Group

The predominant action of this group of drugs (which includes chlorpromazine, promazine and methotrimeprazine) is to inhibit behaviour to varying degrees. They also change the normal hypertensive effect of adrenaline to a hypotensive effect and should, therefore, be avoided when hypotensive drugs are being given.

The most widely used drug in this group is chlorpromazine, which may cause epileptic fits in up to 1 per cent of cases if the doses given are too large or increased too rapidly. Females on this drug are twice as likely as males to develop allergic rashes, angioneurotic oedema and photosensitivity, which disappear with reduced dosage and the administration of antihistamines. Prolonged administration of the drug in high dosage may cause permanent purplish-grey pigmentation on the exposed parts of the skin and a myriad of white dots in the anterior part of the lens capsule and in the cornea. Jaundice, due to intrahepatic obstruction of allergic origin, is more likely to occur in women than men and normally disappears in a few weeks without any residual ill effects.

### b. Piperazine Side-chain Group

This group of drugs (which includes fluphenazine, perphenazine, prochlorperazine, trifluoperazine, thioproperazine and thiopropazate) has a marked effect on the extrapyramidal system and may produce the signs of drug-induced Parkinsonism and various dystonic–dyskinetic reactions and akathisia, which may be very distressing to the patient and alarming to the onlooker. The milder extrapyramidal side-effects can usually be controlled with drugs such as orphenadrine (50–100 mg t.d.s.) or benztropine mesylate (1–4 mg b.d.). The dystonic–dyskinetic reactions may persist for several months after the phenothiazine has been stopped, but may respond to the administration of calcium tablets (1 tablet t.d.s.).

The inability to sit still and the restless pacing up and down, which is characteristic of the patient with akathisia, is apt to be mistaken for the signs of anxiety and to lead to the administration of an increased dosage of the phenothiazine which has caused the condition. The treatment is to change to a non-phenothiazine derivative.

### c. Piperidine Side-chain Group

This group of drugs (which includes thioridazine, pericyazine and pecazine) has less effect on the extrapyramidal system, but is more likely to produce leucopenic–agranulocytic complications, particularly in females over the age of 40.

## 2. NON-PHENOTHIAZINE TRANQUILLIZERS

Haloperidol, a butyrophenone derivative, is very effective in controlling overactivity in mentally subnormal patients, especially children, but occasionally has the opposite effect of increasing overactivity. It is apt to produce extrapyramidal side-effects which can usually be controlled easily with the drugs previously referred to. Claims have been made for the beneficial effects of some anticonvulsant drugs such as sulthiame, beclamide and carbamazine on disturbed behaviour in some non-epileptic mentally subnormal patients.

### 3. *STIMULANTS OF THE CENTRAL NERVOUS SYSTEM*

Amphetamines, normally stimulants of the central nervous system, may produce the paradoxical effect of sedation in some hyperactive mentally subnormal children, who are able to tolerate these drugs in high doses. There is, as yet, no drug with the proved specific direct effect of permanently improving intellectual functioning in the mentally subnormal; although various drugs may do this indirectly by their beneficial effect on accompanying disorders such as depression or epilepsy.

When a drug has been found to improve the behaviour of any mentally subnormal patient, it is very tempting to continue that drug indefinitely, but it should be a general rule to review its use periodically and, if it is not found possible to discontinue it at least temporarily, to ensure that the dose prescribed is the minimum which will produce the therapeutic effect desired. In all cases, it is essential that regular red and white blood counts are carried out if serious, and sometimes fatal, blood dyscrasias are to be avoided. In this connection, when treating anaemia, it should be remembered that the concurrent administration of ferrous sulphate and the tetracyclines by mouth results in a reduction of the plasma level of the latter to only 10–50 per cent of the level expected.

Mentally subnormal patients with superimposed mental illness require the same drugs as those used to treat the illness in people of normal intelligence, e.g. phenothiazines in schizophrenia or tricyclic drugs in depression. Of the latter, amitriptyline has the additional advantage of its sedative action on accompanying anxiety and sleeplessness.

# The Care of
# the Mentally Subnormal

CONSIDERATION as to the best method of care of a mentally subnormal person should follow naturally on the initial multidisciplinary assessment and diagnosis of the underlying condition and be subject to regular review subsequently. The range of services available should be adequate to meet any individual's varying needs at different times.

The question is often asked whether it is better for a mentally subnormal child to be cared for at home or in some sort of residential care elsewhere. The brief answer is that the best place for such a child is in its own home, provided its parents have the intelligence and understanding to give it the particular care it requires and that this be done without sacrificing the rest of the family to the needs of the mentally subnormal child and without adversely affecting the mother's own health.

Some mothers of mentally subnormal children feel a strong sense of guilt (usually without foundation) at having given birth to such a child and feel that they must in some way be to blame. For this reason they attempt to atone for their imagined wrong by sacrificing their own lives and the needs of the rest of the family to the care of the mentally subnormal child, with inevitable disturbance of domestic harmony and often the creation of jealousies and other neurotic disorders in their other children. Such mothers are, of course, themselves in need of psychiatric treatment, directed at removing their underlying sense of guilt and inducing a healthier attitude towards the mentally subnormal child. However, even where the mother's attitude towards the mentally subnormal child is a healthy one, many find it impossible to give it all the care and attention it needs, particularly if it is severely subnormal, faulty in its habits, overactive and destructive, without neglecting the rest of the family. Such parents should be reassured that, under these circumstances, their agreement to hospital care for their mentally subnormal child is not a confession of failure on their part, but, in fact, an enlightened act in the best interests of all the family. They will be helped by the knowledge that they may visit their child in hospital, take it out for the day and have it home for weekends and longer holidays and, if they wish, home for good in due course.

## COMMUNITY CARE

Community care of the mentally subnormal is now the statutory responsibility of local authority social service departments, who may provide residential accommodation for them or undertake their supervision, either on a friendly basis or through the statutory powers of guardianship under the Mental Health Act, 1959. Since the transfer of these latter responsibilities from the local health authorities, the service provided by 'generic' social workers has unfortunately, in many cases, fallen far short of that provided to the mentally subnormal and their families by their specialist mental welfare officer predecessors.

Where it is possible for the mentally subnormal child to be properly cared for at home, it is essential that the parents should have ready access to expert advice on any problems concerning the child, either at the assessment clinic or on a domiciliary basis. Apart from their diagnostic function previously mentioned, the aim of these clinics is to assess patients' abilities and to treat behaviour and other disorders, such as epilepsy, as far as possible on an out-patient basis. They also serve a useful function in the counselling of parents and in helping them to bear what often seems an intolerable burden. The care of the mentally subnormal is very much family psychiatry.

It is important that the mentally subnormal child living at home should receive such education and training as it is capable of benefiting from. Since 1971, this has been the responsibility of the local education authority, who provide special schools and, where possible, home teachers for children who are unable to attend school. Education authorities have power to compel attendance at school, on a daily or a residential basis, of mentally subnormal children of school age, should this be considered to be in the child's interest. For children who are below school age some local authorities provide nursery classes and, for those of school age who are too severely handicapped to attend school, they provide special care units. Some children living at home, attend hospital special schools, which also became the responsibility of local education authorities in 1971, and some of the more severely physically and mentally handicapped attend day hospitals, which are a developing feature of hospital care.

Adult training centres are now the responsibility of local authority social service departments and often include industrial therapy units in which the trainees do simple assembly tasks for local firms, often using specially designed equipment to assist the operation. This work is usually remunerated on a piece-work basis, and in this way the trainee can earn a little pocket money which helps increase his sense of achievement and self-esteem. Some local authorities provide, in addition, training in sheltered workshops in which the conditions are more akin to those in factories, as a preparation for employment in open industry. Trainees are taught the importance of good time-keeping and work habits and the significance of insurance cards, income tax and pension deductions, union membership etc. Some trainees make use also of the adult education facilities provided by local authorities.

The number of hostels and family group homes for both sexes, provided by social service departments for mentally subnormal persons without satisfactory homes, but not requiring hospital care, is increasing but is still far short of what is required to ensure the proper placement of such persons. The same may be said of the provision by social service departments of accommodation for the short-term residential care of mentally subnormal persons living at home, during relatives' holidays or periods of sickness. Sometimes admission to hostels is preceded by a period of treatment and training in hospital. Some local authorities run sponsored lodgings schemes under which they subsidize the cost of keeping mentally subnormal people in approved lodgings.

Many mentally subnormal persons living at home are employed in unskilled or semi-skilled jobs under normal working conditions and with a minimum of supervision from social service departments. Others require much more support than is available at present, although some of them are unwilling to accept it when offered.

Local authorities also provide facilities for indoor and outdoor recreation for mentally subnormal persons living in the community and arrange camps and holidays for them. Some authorities provide clubs for the mentally subnormal, which are run as far as possible on ordinary youth club lines.

Experience of the inevitable difficulties which arise periodically from the existing divisions of responsibility for the care of the mentally subnormal, stresses the necessity for establishing fully integrated services for the mentally subnormal, embracing local authority, hospital and general practitioner services. It is to be hoped that the 1974 reorganization of the National Health Service will find a way of bringing about what goodwill alone has so far failed to achieve.

Valuable contributions to community care are made by various non-statutory and voluntary organizations. Play groups are provided for preschool children, and baby-sitting services enable the parents to take a much-needed break from the care of their children. The principal voluntary organization concerned with the care of the mentally subnormal is the National Society for Mentally Handicapped Children (NSMHC), which provides a wide range of facilities, both residential and non-residential, to supplement those at present provided by statutory authorities, while campaigning for the improvement of the quality and range of existing services by those authorities. The Spastics Society has for some years now recognised the mental

84

handicap of many spastics and is providing education and residential care for them and, like the NSMHC, is actively campaigning for improvement in existing statutory provision. The National Society for Autistic Children has similar aims for children with that specific disability.

The National Association for Mental Health, which pioneered courses for training teachers of mentally handicapped children and the staffs of adult training centres and hospital occupational therapy departments, now the responsibility of statutory authorities, continues to fulfil an invaluable role in organizing a wide range of courses and conferences for professional and lay members in the mental subnormality field and in informing the general public of the needs of the service through its 'Mind' campaign.

Several non-statutory organizations provide long-term residential care for the mentally subnormal in village communities, such as the Camphill villages provided by the Rudolph Steiner Organization, the CARE villages in Devon and Leicestershire, and Ravenswood, a Jewish foundation, in Berkshire.

## HOSPITAL CARE

The following description is based on the procedure in the Stoke Park Group of Hospitals in Bristol, with certain additions.

### 1. MEDICAL CARE

On admission to hospital, the mentally subnormal patient is given a detailed clinical examination, with particular attention to the nervous system and sense organs, to exclude any specific sensory defect such as deafness or blindness. It is important that such sensory defects should not be overlooked as they often suggest a more severe degree of mental subnormality than, in fact, exists, and for this reason, whenever their presence is suspected, expert advice is sought from the ENT and ophthalmic specialist.

X-ray, electro-encephalographic (EEG), air-encephalographic and pathological investigations are carried out as indicated by the clinical findings.

Treatment of any physical disability is instituted as soon as possible, with special attention to any hormonal or nutritional deficiency. A dietician gives advice on both normal and special diets. Orthopaedic abnormalities commonly accompany mental subnormality and are treated by orthopaedic surgeons and may require prolonged physiotherapy. Chiropodists provide an invaluable service, particularly for the older patients.

Dental examination and any necessary treatment, on admission and at regular intervals throughout the patient's stay in hospital, is a routine procedure.

## 2. EDUCATION AND TRAINING

The aim of training is to enable the mentally subnormal patient to develop to the limit of his potentiality, so that eventually he may live outside the hospital, either completely independently or with varying degrees of help and supervision. For the more severely subnormal, of course, this can never be possible and for them the hospital must provide a background of affection, security and stability, and facilities for the full utilization of such abilities as the patients may possess and for their recreational needs. Even some of the most severely subnormal patients have their likes and dislikes of food, staff and companions, and deserve individual consideration. Wherever possible, the severely subnormal patient with gross physical handicap should be got up and dressed each day and provided with toys to stimulate interest and activity. In the hospital for the mentally subnormal, more than any other, should the concept of the therapeutic community be implemented, for in such a hospital a majority of the patients will spend the greater part of their lives.

Before any programme of training is decided upon, the patient is examined by the clinical psychologist, who carries out a full psychological assessment, which includes the discovery of any special abilities or limitations of the patient, such as perceptual disorders, as well as the calculation of his intelligence quotient. The clinical psychologist is also able to provide information concerning the personality structure, which in subnormal patients is often a more important consideration than their relatively mild degree of defect of intelligence alone.

The results of medical and psychological examinations are considered at a case conference attended by medical officers, clinical psychologist, nursing, teaching and occupational therapy staff and social worker who, having seen the patient, plan in broad outline the most suitable programme for him. His case is kept constantly under review at subsequent case conferences, at which the programme is modified according to the patient's progress. These case conferences are invaluable in maintaining the therapeutic community, contributing as they do to the understanding by staff in different departments of the hospital of the needs of each patient and their own contribution to them.

Where patients are admitted to hospital in early childhood the earliest training is habit training, which has often proved impossible at home with so many other demands on the mother's time. If not yet able to walk, they are trained to do so with the help of walking frames and, later, gangways onto which they can hold.

As soon as the patient is mobile, he attends the hospital school, where he is given sense-training to develop the use of the five senses and their integration with each other and the rest of the body. A speech therapist works with the school teacher to remedy the speech defects, which are a frequent accompaniment of mental subnormality, and to overcome, if possible, the special difficulties of the patient who is congenitally deaf through the whole or part of the normal auditory frequency range.

The predominant stress of the school curriculum is on the practical rather than the academic side. Thus, the patient is guided into learning by active participation in a task rather than by purely passive absorption of instruction. Initially this involves various aspects of self-care: dressing and undressing, doing up buttons, washing and brushing his hair and teeth, and tying his shoelaces. This training in school is, of course, inseparable from that given in the ward and, in this respect, the nursing and teaching staff are complementary to each other.

The next stage of training brings the child into contact with the sort of situations with which he will have to deal in later life, and involves skills which the normal child quickly acquires, but which the mentally subnormal child often acquires only after prolonged and painstaking effort—for the severely subnormal child such an apparently simple operation as turning a doorknob may present a considerable problem.

Co-ordination of bodily movements with visual and auditory perception is developed through simple games with balls or bean bags and by taking part in the percussion band. Physical training and country dancing carry this co-ordination further, helping the child to gain self-confidence. Handkerchief drill before these activities and before singing lessons teaches the child this important part of his personal hygiene.

Few severely subnormal patients are capable of benefiting from formal academic subjects, apart from learning to read simple words, to write from a copy, to count mechanically and to do simple problems with money up to about 30 pence. Table-laying is a good exercise for teaching numbers and a shop is a good medium for a child to learn simple weights and measures as well as relative money values. These illustrate well the active method of training encouraged.

Continuity of training is essential in the mentally subnormal if success is to be achieved and, for this reason, the long school holidays of normal schoolchildren are unsuitable, quite apart from the burden they impose on the already-overworked nursing staff.

The simple academic instruction described is supplemented by instruction in handwork, in the usually accepted sense of such activities as painting, modelling, papier-mâché work, knitting and embroidery, as well as in the wider sense of small household tasks such as dusting, filling a jug with water, arranging flowers and emptying and tidying a drawer. For many severely subnormal patients, however, even these activities are beyond them and they are capable only of disorganized play with bricks. Some are unsuitable for attendance at school and teachers hold classes for them on the wards. On the other hand, some mentally subnormal patients show artistic ability and musical and literary appreciation of a standard far higher than their general mental development would suggest.

Children are taken on outings to places of interest such as the zoo. On these occasions, whenever possible, public transport is used and the children are encouraged to tender their own fare to the conductor. A number of children attend the public swimming baths each week and obtain certificates of proficiency in swimming distances up to 1 mile. Others gain a great deal of confidence from regular pony-riding sessions both inside and outside the hospital.

The normal school-leaving age is 16 years but, at the discretion of the head teacher, children may stay on until the age of 19 if they are still benefiting from attendance at school. After this age they may be eligible for the local education authorities' adult education provisions.

At this stage, vocational training is begun for all patients capable of responding to it. The majority of female patients who are employable outside of hospital will obtain work of a domestic nature in either private houses or in hospitals or school canteens. For them, the occupational therapy department runs a domestic science course, which is designed particularly to bridge the gap between life in hospital and that in a private home. Thus, patients are given instruction, for example, in simple cookery, laying the table for different meals, waiting at table, taking messages by telephone, receiving guests, as well as in the use of make-up, in washing, ironing and repairing their own clothing, and in elementary first-aid and in the use of public transport. They are encouraged to make use of the hairdressing salon, where facilities are available for permanent waving as well as regular washing and setting of hair.

Patients are later able to put their knowledge into practice while working, first in the nurses' home, then at a pre-discharge unit attached to the hospital, but remote from it, from which patients go to domestic employment each day, returning to the unit each evening. Ultimately, if their work and behaviour warrant it, they are found residential domestic posts. It is in these daily and residential posts that the patient's training is really consolidated and, far from exploiting the patient as has often been alleged, many employers show extreme tolerance, patience and understanding of her limitations and contribute to her rehabilitation.

Other patients are trained in the hospital laundry for eventual employment in laundries outside. There are, however, many severely subnormal patients who are capable only of the simplest routine domestic work in the sheltered environment of the hospital and who can never reach a high enough standard for outside employment, and others, incapable of outside employment, are employed on repairs in the sewingroom or attend the occupational therapy department each day.

One of the most gratifying and rewarding aspects of hospital care in recent years has been the development and expansion of these occupational therapy departments and the discovery of the previously unsuspected ability in simple handicrafts of patients with mental ages as low as 4 or 5 years. In the past we have been too easily discouraged by the apparent hopelessness of these patients on an initial trial, and have regarded them as unemployable and allowed them to vegetate in the ward, with inevitable mental deterioration and behaviour problems. We now recognize that failure on the initial test is often not an adequate guide to true ability and that with patience and continuity of training, these patients can eventually be taught useful crafts, their behaviour can be improved, and they do not deteriorate so rapidly. However, occupational therapy is very much more than handicrafts alone and embraces many other aspects of the patient's rehabilitation, social training, indoor and outdoor games, remedial gymnastics and outings to places of interest.

The author believes that occupational therapy should be organized in departments separate from the wards and that it should be run by trained occupational therapists rather than by nursing staff, although it is important that student nurses should spend part of their training period in the department. There is no doubt that both patients and nursing staff of the wards benefit from their period of separation during the day. However, for those patients who are unsuitable or unable to attend the occupational therapy department, occupational therapy groups are held on the wards by the nursing staff under the guidance of visiting occupational therapists.

Behaviour modification or operant conditioning techniques are being applied in the case of some of the most severely subnormal or disturbed patients, making use of the giving or withholding of immediate rewards to reinforce desirable habits or eliminate undesirable ones. Claims have been made for the beneficial effect of music therapy with patients of this type.

It must be admitted that it is more difficult to plan definite schemes of vocational training for male patients, as the ultimate types of employment available are less clearly defined than in the case of female patients. However, suitable patients are placed in the hospital's farm training scheme, which attempts in 2 years to provide a graduated training in all aspects of farming with which they might be expected to be familiar if employed as farm labourers. Patients who successfully complete their training are placed in employment on farms or market gardens on either a daily or residential basis, although it has become increasingly difficult to find this sort of employment. Although it is not now fulfilling its original purpose, the farm training scheme is much appreciated by patients and provides an invaluable outlet for the physical energies of some of the more difficult ones, who might otherwise expend them in less socially acceptable activities. It helps to instil regular working habits in these patients, sometimes for the first time in their lives. Patients who do not reach the standard of outside employment continue to work on the hospital farm and grounds and ornamental gardens.

The occupational therapy department for male patients has the same general aims and principles as that for female patients, but the range of crafts is, of course, adapted to the different needs and abilities of male patients, and includes woodwork, mat and basket making, leather and metal work.

Other male patients are employed on domestic work in the wards or assist members of the artisan staff.

When sufficiently stabilized, patients go out to daily employment in private gardens, as porters in markets, unskilled workers in garages, do simple factory work and act as odd-job men in schools, hotels and other places. These patients live in a pre-discharge unit, remote from the main hospital but within the hospital grounds and having easy access to all the recreational facilities of the hospital. It is desirable that patients of this type should be accommodated eventually in their own homes or in private lodgings when they are fit to live outside of hospital. It is unfortunately not certain that members of the general public are yet sufficiently enlightened or tolerant, in spite of their criticism of hospital care, to accept numbers of male mentally subnormal patients living near them in hostels in urban areas, where inevitably they are likely to be blamed, however unjustly, for every unpleasant incident occurring in the neighbourhood. The indiscretions of the female mentally subnormal patient tend to be visited upon herself; those of the male mentally subnormal patient tend to involve other people. The members of the public seem prepared to accept the former, however frequent, but at present not the latter, however rarely they may occur, and tend to judge the behaviour of the majority by that of a very small minority.

Each patient receives pocket money each week, graduated in amount according to his ability to appreciate the value of money.

Extra amounts are given as rewards for work done, whether it be in the occupational therapy department or in playing a more direct part in the working of the hospital, and also as an incentive to good behaviour, liable to be withdrawn should this deteriorate. Patients employed daily outside the hospital, who are earning £3 per week or more, after deductions for income tax, insurance, fares, etc., contribute on a fixed scale to the cost of their maintenance in hospital. Many patients spend their money when out on parole, or in the hospital shop, or save it to buy private clothing for themselves.

Brief reference has already been made to the industrial therapy units which have been developed in recent years, both by local health authorities and in hospitals such as Stoke Park, where our first unit was established in 1957.

Patients with mental ages from about 4 upwards may be employed in such units. They take part, according to their degree of skill, in assembly processes of varying complexity on a piece-work basis for outside firms. Current work includes the assembly and packaging of ballpoint pens and plastic toys and the manufacture of carrier bags. It may take up to 3 months for a patient to learn a process thoroughly, but, once acquired, the skill is freely transferable to other processes which are much more quickly learned.

Few of the patients employed in our industrial therapy units have any real idea of money values, but they understand that the amount they are paid is related to the amount they do. In a time of industrial dispute in the community it was refreshing that our patients wanted to discontinue their tea-break so that they might earn more money in the time devoted to it! It is an additional incentive to them to see the raw materials delivered at the hospital and the completed work collected. They tend to identify themselves with the outside firm concerned. With the money they earn, they buy clothing and other personal articles, which are proudly displayed to visitors. It has been very noticeable how interest in personal appearance improves and how the care of their possessions extends to hospital property and that of other patients.

There has been remarkable improvement in patients' behaviour and manners since the introduction of industrial work. Possibly as a result of working as members of a production team, they have become much more considerate of others in their relationships generally and it has been possible to grant parole to far more than previously and to extend their social activities both inside and outside the hospital.

It is important that the therapeutic purpose of such units should not be sacrificed to industrial efficiency and ever-increasing output, in which the individual needs and problems of each patient are forgotten. For this reason, and to provide variety for patients and staff, and in case the work available should be reduced in trade recession, it is helpful for half a day a week to be devoted to occupational therapy craft work.

A number of patients progress from industrial therapy within the hospital to daily attendance at the Bristol Industrial Therapy Organization (I.T.O.) or at the Spastics Workshops. Although the work done there is very similar to that done previously in hospital, the patients derive great benefit from leaving hospital each day and by the social contact with patients from other hospitals or from the community.

Throughout the patient's stay in hospital, attention is paid to moral, including sexual, instruction. Wherever possible, wards accommodate patients of both sexes, and relationships are encouraged within currently socially acceptable limits, having due regard to each patient's sense of responsibility and the risks of conception. Character training is taught, not only by precept by the hospital staff, but more formally through religious instruction and the discipline of team games for the more active patients.

The mentally subnormal patient is best behaved when fully occupied during his waking hours, and a full recreational programme is arranged for him by full-time recreations organizers. In addition to activities previously mentioned, dances are held for patients of both sexes, television and radio are provided on the wards, and film shows and concert parties are arranged regularly. In some hospitals, patients have their own drama and social clubs. A recent innovation in the Stoke Park Hospital Group has been the introduction of branches of the Women's Institute with a programme of activities within and outside the hospital and full participation in the programmes of other Women's Institutes in the area.

Relatives are encouraged to keep in touch with their children by letter and visits, and to have them home for days, weekends and longer periods during the school holidays. Older patients also spend holidays at home, but for those for whom this is impossible a holiday home at the seaside is provided by the hospital.

Some hospitals have active Parents' Associations and Leagues of Hospital Friends, who make valuable contributions to patient care and entertainment. The primary function of the Stoke Park Hospital League of Friends is to befriend the patient who has no relatives or whose relatives take no interest in him, and to this end they visit or write to the patient regularly and send him greetings cards and presents on his birthday and at Christmas. The less fortunate patients are apt to become jealous if other patients are taken out individually, and, because of this, friends are encouraged to take out small groups and do, frequently, organize coach and pantomime trips. Although, as has been stressed, this is not its primary function, the league is tireless in its efforts to raise money to augment the amenities which can be provided for patients.

In recent years the activities of the League of Friends have been supplemented by those of a wide range of other voluntary organizations, including senior school and student groups, who have made a valuable contribution to the enrichment of the lives of long-stay and severely handicapped patients and to the great enjoyment of the children in camping and other holiday projects. The activities of this very diverse group of volunteers are now coordinated by a Voluntary Services Organizer.

# Intelligence Tests

INTELLIGENCE tests are valuable aids in the assessment of the degree of mental subnormality, but patients should not be classified on the evidence of intelligence tests alone, and attention should always be paid to their former history, including their school and employment record.

According to the psychologist Sir Francis Galton, a person is assumed to have a fund of general native intellectual ability which provides a background against which the more specialized native intellectual abilities operate. These specialized abilities include aptitudes in music, mathematics, creative ability, etc. All psychologists do not agree with Galton's views, but for our purposes they provide a useful working basis.

As will be seen later, some intelligence tests assess mainly general native intellectual ability, whereas others assess chiefly one or other of the specialized native abilities, and the results are dependent in part, at least, on a person's previous education. This ability to acquire knowledge and to profit by experience, however, is an important manifestation of a person's general native intellectual ability. Any test which will assess this general intellectual ability alone is of more assistance in the diagnosis of mental subnormality than tests assessing specialized native intellectual abilities. We all know persons who have marked ability in a special direction whom we would regard as being far from intelligent generally.

The nature of a person's response on testing may provide valuable clues to the presence of brain damage and mental illness.

## STANDARDIZATION OF INTELLIGENCE TESTS

Various tests were applied to large numbers of people of different ages and different classes and, from the marks they scored on each test, an average mark was calculated for each test at each age. That mark was taken as the normal for that particular age and tables were prepared showing the normal mark for each age. Anyone scoring a particular mark is said to have the mental age (MA) corresponding to the chronological age (CA) for which that mark is the normal. By dividing the mental age by the person's chronological age and multiplying the result by 100 a percentage is obtained which is called the intelligence quotient or IQ of that individual. Because native intellectual ability is assumed for the purpose of intelligence tests to have reached the maximum by 15 years of age, in calculating the IQ the chronological age is taken as 15 if the actual age exceeds this. (This does not mean that a person of 15 is as capable of forming sound judgements and of behaving as wisely as an older person, who has had the benefit of greater experience; but rather that the intellectual ability necessary to make best use of experience has normally fully developed by 15 years of age.)

*Examples:*

Mental age $7\frac{1}{2}$ years, chronological age 15 years:
$$IQ = \frac{MA}{CA} \times 100 = \frac{7\frac{1}{2}}{15} \times 100 = 50.$$

Mental age 6 years, chronological age 21 years:
$$IQ = \frac{MA}{CA} \times 100 = \frac{6}{15} \times 100 = 40.$$

It will be seen that a particular mental age corresponds to a particular IQ at each chronological age up to 15 years. In practice, allowance is made in the tables over the age of 15 years for the falling off in some intellectual abilities which is a normal accompaniment of advancing age. However, nowadays IQs are computed by the more accurate deviation method, which does not involve consideration of mental age and which makes an individual's IQs at different ages more strictly comparable.

If many persons are tested and a graph is prepared showing the percentage of the total gaining each IQ, the curve appears roughly as shown overleaf, with slightly more individuals at the lower end of the IQ range than at the upper end, due to the effect of non-genetic causes of impaired intelligence. If the distribution of intelligence depended entirely on genetic factors, the curve would be completely symmetrical about its mid-point, with the percentage of individuals with IQs less than 25 equal to that of individuals with IQs over 160.

About half the population have IQs within the range of 90 and 110. There is no sharp dividing line in terms of IQ between normal and subnormal intelligence, but current clinical practice sets the upper limits of subnormality at about an IQ of 70 to 80, depending upon the particular test used. Equally, there is no sharp dividing line in terms of IQ between subnormality and severe subnormality, but, in practice, individuals with IQs up to 60 may fall within the legal definition of severe subnormality when they are first classified under the Mental Health Act, 1959 (which is the only basis for distinguishing between what are essentially legal, rather than clinical, categories). It must be stressed again, however, that in the present imperfect state of intelligence tests, the IQ cannot be regarded as a rigid criterion for the diagnosis of subnormality or severe subnormality.

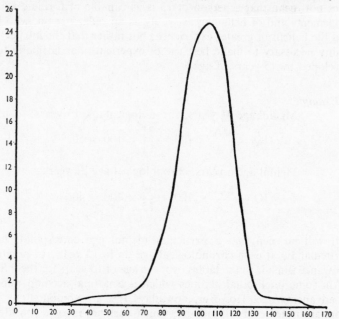

## TYPES OF INTELLIGENCE TESTS

Intelligence tests as a whole may be divided into verbal and performance tests; but a particular battery of tests may assess both these aspects of intellectual ability.

Some of the tests are suitable for testing a number of persons at one time; this is referred to as 'group testing'; others can be applied only to individuals.

The tests in most general use at the present time are as follows:
1. Wechsler Intelligence Test.
2. Stanford–Binet Intelligence Test as revised by Terman–Merrill (Form L–M).
3. Raven's Matrices.
4. Porteus Maze.
5. Kent Oral Test.

6. Merrill–Palmer Test.
7. Drever–Collins Test.

## 1. WECHSLER INTELLIGENCE TEST

There are two separate scales in this test—the Wechsler Intelligence Scale for Children (WISC) for testing children between the ages of 5 and 15 years and the Wechsler Adult Intelligence Scale (WAIS) for testing persons between the ages of 10 and 60 years.

The Wechsler test is really a battery of tests, each of which has been shown from wide application to give reliable results. The complete battery consists of the following ten tests:

### a. INFORMATION TEST

A person's score on this test obviously depends on his educational and cultural opportunities, and as such might not be considered to give a true indication of native intellectual ability. It has been found, however, that the range of a man's knowledge is usually a very good indication of his general native intellectual ability and is an indication of his alertness towards the world around him. It is, however, a poor test for those deprived of the opportunity of receiving verbal information.

A person's score declines less with age on this test than on any other test.

### b. COMPREHENSION TEST

This may best be described as a test of common sense, which is a good reflection of general native intellectual ability. In addition, this test provides valuable clinical data about the subject, and a good indication of his personality may often be gained from the mode of his responses.

Persons who are unaccustomed to putting their ideas into words are handicapped on this test.

Scores on this test hold up well with age.

### c. ARITHMETICAL REASONING

This test is an indication of a person's alertness, but it is obviously influenced by education and occupation and the result is affected by fluctuations of attention and by transient emotional reactions. Although dependent in part on specialized native intellectual ability, the results of this test are, in persons of mentally subnormal level at least, a good indication of general native intellectual ability.

Test scores fall with age.

## d. MEMORY SPAN FOR DIGITS

This is a test of retentiveness, but a poor test of general native intellectual ability. However, like the previous test, it is good at the lower levels of intelligence and is helpful in picking out the severely subnormal, who are often unable to repeat five digits forwards or three backwards.

This test may also reveal temperamental traits such as lack of attention or concentration.

Test scores fall rapidly with age.


## e. SIMILARITIES TEST

This test provides a good indication of the logic of a person's thinking processes and is a very good indication of general native intellectual ability. The mentally subnormal may grasp superficial likeness, but they are usually quite unable to discern essential likeness.

In addition, the nature of the subject's responses may provide valuable indications as to his personality.

Test scores hold up fairly well with age.


## f. PICTURE ARRANGEMENT TEST

This measures the subject's ability to comprehend and size up a total situation. The subject is required to rearrange a dissected comic strip so as to tell a story. Its value, therefore, varies according to the subject's interest in the content of the strip. It does, however, give a fair indication of a person's general native intellectual ability.

Test scores hold up badly with age.


## g. PICTURE COMPLETION TEST

This measures an individual's basic ability to distinguish essential from inessential details.

The subject is required to name the part missing from an incomplete picture. The results depend in part on the subject's previous experience and familiarity with the picture presented, but this is a useful test at the lower end of the intelligence scale for indicating general native intellectual ability. It discriminates poorly, however, at higher levels of intelligence.

Test scores hold up well with age.

## h. BLOCK DESIGN

This is the best of the Wechsler performance tests. It assesses the ability to recognize and reproduce designs and is an excellent test of general native intellectual ability.

The test is a modification of the Kohs block test.

Useful additional evidence of temperamental traits may be gleaned by watching the patient's attitude and emotional reactions while performing the test.

Test scores do not hold up well with age.

## i. DIGIT SYMBOL TEST

This is a test of the subject's perceptual ability, but is also dependent on a manual factor. The subject is required to reproduce the unfamiliar symbols which are associated in the key with particular numerals. This test cannot, therefore, be used on illiterates who are not used to handling pencils and paper. In others, however, this manual factor is of importance in that the speed and accuracy with which the subject performs the test give a good indication of general native intellectual ability.

Test scores decline rapidly with age.

## j. OBJECT ASSEMBLY TEST

This, also, is a test of perceptual ability and of the subject's reaction to the whole and of his ability to form a critical understanding of the relationship of the individual parts. The subject is required to piece together three sets to form a mannikin, a profile and a hand, but is not told the nature of the completed object before the test.

This is more a qualitative test of the subject's thinking and working habits than a reliable quantitative test of general native intellectual ability.

## VOCABULARY TEST

This serves as an alternative test. Contrary to general belief, the size of one's vocabulary is an excellent indication of one's general native intellectual ability as well as being an index of one's education, and serves as a measure of one's learning ability.

Test scores hold up better than those on most other tests in the battery, but do fall off somewhat with age.

The complete battery of tests may be given or, if time does not permit, the first five only. Tables are provided with the Wechsler battery of tests to enable the 'raw' score on each individual test to be modified so as to be comparable with the scores on each of the other tests in the battery. These so-called 'weighted scores' are added up and the IQ is read from the tables for the appropriate age group.

The Wechsler battery of tests has been described in some detail in order to indicate as far as possible the purpose of various kinds of tests. The other tests listed above differ in content rather than in principle from those of the Wechsler series. They will, therefore, be described only briefly.


## 2. STANFORD–BINET TEST

This was originally a French test but has been revised by the Americans Terman and Merrill and further slightly modified for use in this country. There are tests for each year of life from 2 to 14 years, atest for the average adult and three tests for superior adults.

There is a test for each 6-monthly period from 2 to 4 years, in each of which there are six subtests. Each subtest is intended to correspond roughly with 1 month of the child's life between these ages. Between 5 and 14 years there are six subtests for each 12-monthly period, so that in this age group each subtest corresponds roughly with a 2-monthly period.

The subject is first given the test corresponding to 2 years below his chronological age and then those for successive years, until no further response is obtained. For each year's test completed, he is credited with the mental age of that year and with an additional mental age of 1/12 for each subtest passed between 2 and 4 years and an additional 2/12 for each subtest between 5 and 14 years, where he has failed to pass the complete test for those years. The total so obtained is regarded as the subject's 'mental age' (MA). Additional credits are given to subjects passing all or part of the various adult tests.

Tables are provided with the Stanford–Binet test to convert the mental age to the intelligence quotient.

The Stanford–Binet test, even in its revised form, is said to penalize the mentally subnormal in the subcultural group as it is so heavily weighted with verbal and educational items. The WAIS is considered a more appropriate test for application to this group.


## 3. RAVEN'S MATRICES

This is a perceptual test of intelligence and is claimed to give a good assessment of general native intellectual ability without invoking social training, educational status or muscular co-ordination and speed. The subject is required to select the correct pattern, from a number of alternatives, to complete a design.

## 4. PORTEUS MAZE

This consists of a series of mazes of increasing complexity, there being one maze for each year of life from 3 to 14 years with the exception of year 13, for which there is no maze. There are two mazes for adults. The subject is credited with the mental age corresponding to the most difficult maze traced. Additional credit is given for completing the adult mazes. The mental ages so obtained on this test, however, are only approximate and too much reliance should not be placed on them.

## 5. KENT ORAL TEST

This is a quick test, which is useful for revealing obvious mental subnormality, and consists of a series of fairly simple questions, but of increasing difficulty, ranging from 'What are houses made of?' to 'If your shadow points to the north-east where is the sun?'

## 6. MERRILL–PALMER TEST

This test is part verbal and part performance. It is, however, liable to give false results owing to social training influences, but it is useful for testing children who are thought to be mentally subnormal.

## 7. DREVER–COLLINS TEST

This is a performance test specially adapted for testing deaf persons who cannot comprehend spoken instructions.

## TESTS SUGGESTED FOR USE WITH PRESUMED MENTALLY SUBNORMAL PERSONS

| Approximate chronological age years | Test |
|---|---|
| 0–3 | None worth doing |
| 3–7 | Merrill–Palmer |
| 7–17 | Stanford–Binet |
| 8–17 | Matrices 1947 (for children 5–9 years of age normally, but can be used as check in this group). Matrices 1938 (mentally subnormal persons over 12 years) |
| 5–15 | WISC |
| 15–60 | WAIS |
| 14 upwards | Matrices 1938 Various performance tests |

There is also a Wechsler Test specially adapted for use with blind persons.

At any age from 5 years upwards, assistance may be gained from the child's school reports.

## DEVELOPMENTAL SCALES

### 1. GESELL DEVELOPMENTAL SCHEDULES

There is one schedule for infants up to the age of 36 months and one for the preschool child from the age of 15 months up to 6 years. These schedules provide standards of normal development of motor activity, language, adaptive behaviour and social behaviour at various ages within the above limits. They provide useful indications of progress when formal intelligence tests cannot be applied.

### 2. GRIFFITHS DEVELOPMENTAL SCHEDULES

The tests in these schedules were modified from those of Gesell to provide a general intelligence quotient (GQ), based on the average of quotients obtained in each of five fields of development: locomotion, personal social, speech, hand and eye, and performance (which includes the ability to reason and to manipulate material intelligently).

### 3. VINELAND SOCIAL MATURITY SCALE

The importance of a mentally subnormal person's social sense has been stressed above, and the Vineland Social Maturity Scale is an attempt to assess this objectively from a consideration of his behaviour. The scale covers the period from birth to about 25 years, but is more useful at younger ages.

Although too much reliance cannot be placed on the results obtained from this test, they serve as useful indications of progress made as a result of training in hospital.

Each item on this scale is conceived as representing a definite step in the development of the sense of social responsibility and is expressed in some detailed performance. Consequently, the value of the detailed items is determined principally by the extent to which they reflect the growth of personal independence.

### 4. GUNZBURG PROGRESS ASSESSMENT CHARTS OF SOCIAL DEVELOPMENT

These charts record development under four headings: self-help, communication, socialization and occupation. A number of skills are included under each of these headings, and the charts are designed to enable easy visual comparison of those skills present on initial recording with those present on subsequent occasions, and to identify specific weaknesses.

Separate charts are used for different age groups and levels of functioning: the Primary Progress Assessment Chart (PPAC) for very young normal children and for the profoundly mentally handicapped child and adult, the Progress Assessment Chart 1 (PAC 1) for the age group 6–16 years (there is a modified form (M/PAC 1) in which the special learning difficulties of the child with Down's syndrome are taken into consideration) and the Progress Assessment Chart 2 (PAC 2), for use with teenagers and older mentally handicapped people.

A Progress Evaluation Index has been developed for use with each Progress Assessment Chart, to enable the achievements of an individual on that chart to be compared with the average attainments of other mentally handicapped people of comparable intelligence.

## PERSONALITY TESTS

As has been pointed out, some intelligence tests, as well as revealing intellectual ability, give interesting indications as to the subject's personality. To explore this field further, however, special personality or projection tests have been devised. In the Rorschach Blot Test, the subject is shown a series of ink-blots and is asked what each suggests to him. In the Szondi Test, he is asked to choose from a number of photographs of human faces those which, in his opinion, fulfil criteria suggested by the examiner, and in the Repertory Grid Test to rate each of eight pictures for various undesirable characteristics. The Eysenck–Withers Test is a test of extroversion, introversion and neuroticism, and is dependent on the subject's ability to read the instructions and, therefore, has limited use in the mentally subnormal.

Such tests are undoubtedly useful, but it is claimed by some critics that the interpretation of results is often too dependent on the examiner's own personality.

A useful projection test for the mentally subnormal is based on the Lowenfeld World Technique. The patient is provided with a sand-tray and toy equipment: fences, trees, buildings, transport, animals, people, etc. and is asked to make whatever he likes with these materials. Personality traits and disturbances are revealed in the form of the world the patient builds.

# Legal Aspects of the Care
# of the Mentally Handicapped

THE Mental Health Act, 1959, for all practical purposes, is applicable only to England and Wales, and all references to sections of that Act apply to all types of mental disorder except where specifically stated.

The Mental Health (Scotland) Act, 1960, will be outlined in the following chapter, in which reference will be made also to the Mental Health Act (Northern Ireland), 1961.

Various sections of these Acts have been repealed or amended by subsequent legislation. These sections are indicated below, and the effect of the subsequent legislation is stated at the end of the first relevant section.

## THE MENTAL HEALTH ACT, 1959

### PART I

Section 2 effects the dissolution of the Board of Control.
Section 3 establishes in place of the Board of Control

### MENTAL HEALTH REVIEW TRIBUNALS

Under the Mental Health Act, 1959, there is one Mental Health Review Tribunal for each Regional Hospital Board Area.

Each Tribunal consists of *legal members* approved by the Lord Chancellor, *medical members* appointed by the Lord Chancellor after consultation with the Minister of Health and a *number of other persons* appointed by the Lord Chancellor, after consultation with the Minister, as having such experience in administration, such knowledge of social services or such other qualifications or experience as the Lord Chancellor considers suitable.

The *Chairman* of the Tribunal is appointed by the Lord Chancellor and *must be a legal member*.

For the purposes of any proceedings under the Mental Health Act, 1959, a Mental Health Review Tribunal must consist of a *minimum of three persons* appointed by the Chairman: one from the legal members, one from the medical members and one from the members who are neither legal nor medical members. If the Chairman is unable himself for any reason to appoint the members, this function is carried out by another member appointed by the Chairman for this purpose and, in the absence of the Chairman, one of the other legal members nominated by him acts as *President* of the Tribunal.

A member of a Mental Health Review Tribunal for one area may be appointed to serve on a Mental Health Review Tribunal for any other area as though he were a member of the other Tribunal.

# PART II
## *LOCAL AUTHORITY SERVICES*
### Functions of Local Health Authority

SECTION 6. This section confirms local health authorities' functions, under section 28 of the National Health Service Act, 1946, to provide residential accommodation for the care and aftercare of mentally disordered persons, to provide occupation and training facilities for them, and to undertake their guardianship under the Mental Health Act, 1959. It also authorizes the local health authority to appoint officers to act as *mental welfare officers* for the purpose of the Act.

(N.B. This section was repealed by the Health Services and Public Health Act, 1968, and local health authorities' responsibilities have been transferred from local authorities' Health Departments to their Social Services Departments by the Local Authority Social Services Act. 1970.)

SECTION 10. This section requires the local health authority to visit, in hospital or nursing home, mentally disordered children or young persons, where parental rights have been assumed by the Children's Department of the local authority, mentally disordered persons subject to their guardianship, and those whose nearest relatives' rights have been transferred to the local health authority. (*See* note on section 6.)

### Duty of Local Education Authority

SECTIONS 11–13. These sections were repealed by the Education (Handicapped Children) Act, 1970, which made local education authorities responsible for providing education for all children of school age, *irrespective of their level of intelligence.*

# PART III
## *MENTAL NURSING HOMES AND RESIDENTIAL HOMES*

SECTIONS 14–17. These sections impose on the local health authorities responsibility for the registration and inspection of '*mental nursing homes'* in their area, to ensure that conditions imposed by the local health authority itself or by the Minister are being fulfilled.

The local authority is authorized (section 22) to inspect also premises registered under the National Assistance Act, 1948, as a residential home for mentally disordered persons, if at any time it has reasonable cause to believe that any mentally disordered patient therein is not under proper care.

## HOSPITAL CARE AND GUARDIANSHIP

### Informal Admission of Patients to Hospital

SECTION 5. This section *permits* the informal admission to any hospital or mental nursing home of any patient who requires treatment for mental disorder. By inference from subsection 2 of this section, a patient informally admitted may be detained in hospital at his parents' or guardian's request until the age of 16 years, whatever his own wishes in the matter may be. However, there is no provision in the Act for the detention in hospital of an informally admitted severely subnormal person (who is by definition incapable of living an independent life or of guarding himself against serious exploitation) over the age of 16 years, for even a few hours, pending the making of alternative arrangements for his care outside hospital. This, in the author's submission, is a real defect of the Act, which could lead to charges of wrongful detention if this section were strictly interpreted. Experience in the past has suggested that strict legal interpretations are considered to be more important than a patient's welfare.

## PART IV

### COMPULSORY ADMISSION TO HOSPITAL AND RECEPTION INTO GUARDIANSHIP

#### Admission for Observation

SECTION 25. This section *authorizes the detention in hospital for observation* (with or without other medical treatment), *for a period not exceeding twenty-eight days*, of any patient suffering from a mental disorder, *provided* it can be shown that his mental disorder warrants this and that it is in the interests of his own health or safety or of the protection of others.

SECTION 27. An *application for admission for observation* may be made to the managers of the hospital either *by the nearest relative* or *by a mental welfare officer* who must have seen the patient personally within a period of fourteen days ending with the date of the application.

Section 28. The application has to be founded on the *written recommendations* in the prescribed form, signed on or before the date of application, *of two medical practitioners* who have personally examined the patient either together or at an interval of not more than seven days. One of these medical recommendations must be given by a practitioner approved by the local health authority as having special experience in the diagnosis or treatment of mental disorder. Unless this practitioner has himself previous acquaintance with the patient the other recommendation must, if practicable, be given by a medical practitioner with such acquaintance. The recommendations may be given either separately or as a joint recommendation signed by both practitioners (section 27).

The patient must be admitted to hospital within a period of fourteen days, beginning with the date on which he was last examined by a practitioner before giving his medical recommendation (section 31).

Except where the application is for admission to a mental nursing home or to private beds in a hospital, *one* of the medical recommendations may be given by a practitioner on the staff of the hospital to which the patient is to be admitted. In addition to these limitations a medical recommendation may not be given by any of the following persons:

1. The applicant.
2. A partner of the applicant or of a practitioner by whom another medical recommendation is given for the purposes of the same application.
3. A person employed as an assistant by the applicant or by any such practitioner as aforesaid.
4. A person who receives or has an interest in the receipt of any payments made on account of the maintenance of the patient, or by the husband, wife, father, father-in-law, mother, mother-in-law, son, son-in-law, daughter, daughter-in-law, brother, brother-in-law, sister, sister-in-law of the patient or of any such person as aforesaid, or of a practitioner by whom another medical recommendation is given for purposes of the same application.

## Admission for Treatment

Section 26. This section *authorises the detention in hospital for treatment* (in the first instance, *for a period not exceeding one year* (section 43)), of a patient of *any* age suffering from *mental illness* or *severe* subnormality; or from *psychopathic disorder* or *subnormality if under the age of 21 years, provided* that it can be shown that his mental state warrants this and that it is in the interests of his own health or safety or of the protection of others.

SECTION 27. An *application for admission for treatment* under section 26 may be made either *by the nearest relative* (as defined in section 49) of the patient or *by a mental welfare officer* after consultation with the nearest relative (and *not against his expressed objection*), unless consultation is not reasonably practicable or would involve unreasonable delay. The applicant must have seen the patient personally within a period of fourteen days ending with the date of the application and must, if the patient is suffering from psychopathic disorder or subnormality, state his age or that he is believed to be under the age of 21 years if his exact age is not known.

SECTION 28. In addition to the general requirements as to *medical recommendations* under the application for observation procedure, described above, the following requirements apply specifically in the case of the application for admission for treatment procedure under section 26:

The recommendation must state whether other methods of dealing with the patient are available, and if so why they are not appropriate. Both recommendations must describe the patient as suffering from the *same one* form of mental disorder, although either or both may describe him as suffering from other forms in addition.

The patient must be admitted to hospital within a period of fourteen days, beginning with the date on which he was last examined by a practitioner before giving his medical recommendation (section 31).

The patient may apply to a *Mental Health Review Tribunal* within a period of six months beginning with the day of his admission or with the day on which he attains the age of 16 years, whichever is the later (section 31).

### Admission for Observation in Case of Emergency

SECTION 29. This section authorizes *the mental welfare officer* or *any relative of the patient*, in any case of urgent necessity, to apply for the patient's detention in hospital for observation under section 25 if full compliance with the provisions of that section would involve unreasonable delay. The applicant must have seen the patient personally within a period of three days ending with the date of the application.

The application may be founded on *one* medical recommendation only, given, if practicable, by a practitioner with previous acquaintance with the patient and signed on or before the date of the application.

The patient must be admitted to hospital within a period of three days beginning with the date on which he was examined by the medical practitioner giving the medical recommendation, or with the date of the application, whichever is the earlier (section 31).

108

Under this emergency procedure a *patient may be detained for seventy-two hours only*, unless a second medical recommendation (subject to the limitations defined in section 28 as regards the practitioner's relationship with the applicant or the practitioner giving the other recommendation) is given and received by the managers within that period.

## Applications in Respect of Patients already in Hospital

SECTION 30. This section *authorizes the detention in hospital for a period of three days of an informal admission*, on the written report to the managers of the hospital by the *responsible medical officer* (the medical practitioner in charge of the case), that it appears to him that an application should be made for the patient's admission to hospital under one of the compulsory procedures in earlier sections.

## *GUARDIANSHIP*

SECTION 33. This section *authorizes the reception into the guardianship* of either a local health authority or of any other person, including the applicant himself, approved by the local health authority, of any person suffering from mental disorder which warrants his reception into guardianship, *provided* that it is in the interests of the patient or for the protection of other persons. The same age limits apply in psychopathic disorder or subnormality as in the case of applications for admission for hospital treatment under section 26 and also the same general provisions as to applications and medical recommendations. However, in the case of guardianship, the application is made to the local health authority named as guardian or to the local health authority for the area in which the person named resides, with a statement that he is willing to act as guardian. (*See* note on section 6.)

SECTION 34. The *application* has to be forwarded to the local health authority within a period of fourteen days beginning with the date on which the patient was last examined by a medical practitioner before giving a medical recommendation. If accepted by the local health authority the application immediately confers on the authority or person named as guardian the same powers over the patient as would be the case if they or he were the father of the patient and the patient were under the age of 14 years. (*See* note on section 6.)

The patient may apply to a *Mental Health Review Tribunal* within a period of six months beginning with the day on which the application is accepted, or with the day on which he attains the age of 16 years, whichever is the later.

**Patient's Correspondence**

SECTION 36. This section authorizes the responsible medical officer (*and no one else*) to withhold from a patient detained in hospital any postal packet addressed to him if it is calculated to interfere with the patient's treatment or to cause him unnecessary distress.

The responsible medical officer is required to return the packet to the sender if he can be identified.

The section also authorizes the responsible medical officer to withhold from the Post Office any postal packet addressed by a patient detained in hospital, either if the addressee has specifically requested this in writing to the managers of the hospital or to the responsible medical officer, or if it appears to the responsible medical officer that the packet would be unreasonably offensive to the addressees, or is defamatory of other persons (*other than persons on the staff of the hospital*), or would be likely to prejudice the interests of the patient. No one, apart from the responsible medical officer, has any authority to open and examine a postal packet from a patient detained in hospital and he may do so only if, in his opinion, the patient's mental disorder is calculated to lead him to send a communication of the type referred to. However, *no one* has any authority to open, examine or withhold from the Post Office a postal packed addressed to any of the following:

1. The Minister.
2. Any Member of the Commons House of Parliament.
3. The Master or Deputy Master or any other officer of the Court of Protection.
4. The managers of the hospital.
5. Any other authority or person having power to discharge the patient (apart from authorities or persons with powers of discharge of patients concerned in criminal proceedings only).
6. A Mental Health Review Tribunal: at any time the patient is entitled to apply to that Tribunal and to any other class of persons as the Minister may prescribe by regulations.

The provisions of this section apply similarly to *patients undergoing treatment informally* in hospital or in a mental nursing home (section 134) and to *patients subject to guardianship*, with the substitution of 'guardian' for 'managers of the hospital' and 'guardian or any other person authorised by the guardian' for 'responsible medical officer'.

## *LEAVE OF ABSENCE FROM HOSPITAL*

SECTION 39. This section *authorizes the responsible medical officer to grant, for any period, leave of absence* to a patient liable to be detained in hospital, subject to any conditions he considers necessary in the interests of the patient or for the protection of other persons,

110

including the requirement that the patient shall remain during his absence in the custody of any person authorized in writing by the managers of the hospital.

A patient may not be recalled to hospital from leave of absence after he has ceased to be liable to be detained in hospital, or *after the expiration of the period of six months* beginning with the first day of his absence on leave, *provided* he has not returned to hospital or been transferred to another hospital under the provisions of the Mental Health Act during this period and *provided* he is not absent without leave at the expiration of this period.

## ABSENCE WITHOUT LEAVE

SECTION 40. This section *authorizes the taking into custody and the return to hospital,* by any mental welfare officer or any officer on the staff of the hospital, any constable or any person authorized in writing by the managers of the hospital, of any patient absent without leave from the hospital or failing to return to the hospital at the expiration of a period of authorized leave or if recalled from leave or absenting himself without permission from any place where he is required to reside as a condition of leave.

Similarly, this section *authorizes the taking into custody and return to his required place of residence,* by any officer on the staff of a local health authority, by any constable or by any person authorised in writing by the guardian or a local health authority, of any patient subject to guardianship who absents himself without the leave of his guardian from his required place of residence. (*See* note on section 6.)

Psychopathic and subnormal patients *over the age of twenty-one* on the first day of absence without leave may be dealt with in this way at any time *within a period of six months* beginning with that day, but *in any other case* this period is limited to *twenty-eight days.* After these periods have expired the patient ceases to be liable to be detained or subject to guardianship.

## TRANSFER OF PATIENTS

SECTION 41. This section *authorizes the continued detention of patients liable to detention when they are transferred from one hospital to another,* the *transfer to the guardianship of another local health authority* (or of any person approved by such an authority) *of any person subject to guardianship,* or the *transfer into guardianship of a patient liable to detention in hospital, or vice versa.* (*See* note on section 6.)

A patient who has attained the age of 16 years, transferred from guardianship to hospital in this way, may apply to a *Mental Health*

*Review Tribunal* within the period of six months beginning with the day on which he is transferred.

If a guardian dies or is unwilling to continue as guardian the guardianship of the patient thereupon rests in the local authority pending the appointment of another guardian. The functions of a guardian, temporarily incapacitated by illness or any other cause, may be transferred during his incapacity to the local health authority or any other person approved by that authority. (*See* note on section 6.)

A County Court, on application by a mental welfare officer, may order that the guardianship of a patient be transferred to a local health authority or to any other person approved by that authority, if it appears that the current guardian has performed his functions negligently or in a manner contrary to the interests of the patient (section 42). (*See* note on section 6.)

## DURATION OF AUTHORITY FOR DETENTION OR GUARDIANSHIP AND DISCHARGE OF PATIENTS

SECTION 43. This section *limits the authority for detention in hospital or under guardianship to a period not exceeding one year*, beginning with the day the patient was admitted to hospital or the guardianship application accepted. However, it authorizes the detention or guardianship for a *further period of one year*, and, *subsequently, for periods of two years* at a time if, within a period of two months ending with the last day of these periods, the responsible medical officer reports to the managers of the hospital, or if the nominated medical attendant of a patient under guardianship reports to the responsible local health authority in the prescribed form, that continued detention is necessary in the interests of the patient's health or safety or for the protection of others or that guardianship is necessary in the interests of the patient or for the protection of other persons.

The managers or local health authority are required to notify patients over the age of 16 years of each renewal of authority and the patient may apply to a *Mental Health Review Tribunal* within the period for which the authority is renewed. (*See* note on section 6.)

## SPECIAL PROVISIONS AS TO PSYCHOPATHIC AND SUBNORMAL PATIENTS

SECTION 44. This section *terminates the authority for detention or guardianship* of a psychopathic or subnormal patient upon his attaining the age of 25 years, *unless*, in the case of a patient detained in hospital, the responsible medical officer, within the period of two months ending on the patient's twenty-fifth birthday, furnishes to the managers a report in the prescribed form that it appears to him that

112

the *patient would be likely to act in a manner dangerous to other persons or to himself* if released from hospital.

The managers are required to inform the patient and nearest relative of this report, and both have the right, within a period of twenty-eight days beginning with the patient's twenty-fifth birthday, to apply to the *Mental Health Review Tribunal.*


## DISCHARGE OF PATIENTS

SECTION 47. This section *authorizes the following persons to make an order discharging a patient from detention or guardianship:*

The *responsible medical officer* or the *managers of the hospital* in the case of a patient detained in hospital for *observation.*

The *responsible medical officer*, the *managers of the hospital* or the *nearest relative* in the case of a patient detained for *treatment.*

The *responsible medical officer*, the *responsible local health authority* or the *nearest relative* in the case of a patient subject to *guardianship.*

The *registration authority* in the case of a patient liable to be detained in a *mental nursing home* for *observation* or *treatment* or the *Regional Hospital Board* (Area Health Authority after 1 April, 1974) if the patient is maintained there under a contract with that Board.

All these powers may be exercised by *any three or more members* of the authorities authorized to act on their behalf. (*See* note on section 6.)


## RESTRICTIONS ON DISCHARGE BY THE NEAREST RELATIVE

SECTION 48. This section *requires the nearest relative to give not less than seventy-two hours' notice in writing* to the managers of the hospital *of an order to discharge a patient liable to detention in hospital* and *authorizes the continued detention of the patient, against the nearest relative's wishes,* if the responsible medical officer reports to the managers, *within the period of notice,* that in his opinion the patient would be *likely to act in a manner dangerous to others or himself if discharged.* It also denies the relative the right to order discharge again *during a period of six months* beginning with the date of the responsible medical officer's report, but requires the relative to be informed of the report and confers on him the right to apply to a *Mental Health Review Tribunal* within the period of twenty-eight days beginning with the day on which he was informed.

SECTION 52. This section *authorizes a County Court,* upon application, *to order that the functions of the nearest relative be transferred,* under circumstances defined in the section, to any other person

113

specified in the application, who, in the opinion of the Court, is a proper person to act as the patient's nearest relative.

Such an application may be made by *any* relative of the patient, by any other person with whom the patient is residing or was last residing before admission to hospital, or by a mental welfare officer.

This section *confers on the nearest relative* of a patient liable to detention or subject to guardianship the *right to apply to a Mental Health Review Tribunal* within the period of twelve months beginning with the date of the order under this section and in any subsequent period of twelve months.


## PART V

### ADMISSION OF PATIENTS CONCERNED IN CRIMINAL PROCEEDINGS AND TRANSFER OF PATIENTS UNDER SENTENCE

SECTION 60. This section *authorizes a Court of Assize or Quarter Sessions* (in the case of a person convicted of an offence other than one for which the sentence is fixed by law) or a *Magistrates' Court* (in the case of a person convicted of an offence punishable on summary conviction) *to order that person's admission to, and detention in, a specified hospital or to place him under the guardianship of a local health authority* or of any other specified person approved by a local health authority, *provided* that the Court is satisfied on the written or oral evidence of *two* medical practitioners that the offender is suffering from mental illness, psychopathic disorder, subnormality or severe subnormality which warrants this, and that, having regard to all the circumstances, this is the most suitable method of dealing with the case. The Court must also be satisfied that the hospital specified will be able to admit the patient within a period of twenty-eight days beginning with the date of the making of the order, or that the local health authority or other person specified is willing to receive the offender into guardianship. (*See* note on section 6.)

A *Magistrates' Court* may make an order under this section of the Act *without convicting a person* suffering from mental illness or *severe* subnormality *provided* the Court is satisfied he did the act.

(N.B. As a result of the Courts Act, 1971, the powers of the Courts of Assize and Quarter Sessions were transferred to Crown Courts.)

SECTION 61. This section *authorizes a Juvenile Court* (in the case of a child or young person brought before the Court under section 62 or section 64 of the Children and Young Persons Act, 1938) *to make a hospital order or guardianship order*, *provided* that the Court is satisfied that the child or young person is in need of care or protection, or that his parent or guardian is unable to control him and that the

114

conditions which are required under section 60 for the making of a hospital order or guardianship order are, so far as is applicable, satisfied in the case of the child or young person.

The Court must also be satisfied that the *parent or guardian understands* the results which will follow from the order and *consents* to its being made.

(N.B. This section was repealed by the Children's and Young Persons Act, 1969, and the Juvenile Courts' power to make a hospital or guardianship order is now conferred by section 1 (3) of that Act.)

SECTION 63. This section *cancels the power of the nearest relative to order discharge of a patient admitted to hospital as a result of a Court order* and *removes the age limits to the detention of psychopathic and subnormal patients in hospital or under guardianship.* However, it *authorizes the patient to apply to a Mental Health Review Tribunal* within the period of six months beginning with the date of the order or with the day on which he attains the age of 16 years, whichever is the later, and *authorizes the nearest relative to make a similar application* within the period of twelve months beginning with the date of the order and in any subsequent period of twelve months.

SECTION 64. This section *authorizes the patient's detention in a place of safety pending his admission to hospital within a period of twenty-eight days* beginning with the day on which the hospital order was made by the Court.

SECTION 65. This section *authorizes a Court of Assize or Quarter Sessions to impose an order restricting the patient's discharge and any of the following special restrictions,* either indefinitely or for a specified period, where this is considered necessary for the protection of the public, *provided* that the medical evidence of *at least one* of the medical practitioners was given *orally* in Court. (*See* note on section 60.)

During the period that discharge is restricted, the normal limit to the duration of the authority for detention does not apply and *no application can be made to the Mental Health Review Tribunal.*

The *consent of the Secretary of State is necessary* before the patient can be transferred to another hospital or to guardianship or vice versa or before he can be granted leave, and he can be recalled from leave at any time while the order restricting discharge is in force. The Secretary of State's consent is also necessary before the patient may be discharged by any of the persons who normally have this power.

Unfortunately, courts do not always ascertain, before making an order under section 65, that the receiving hospital is able to implement its requirements. *These requirements are, in the author's view, inappropriate in an open hospital which is trying to follow a therapeutic rather than custodial role.*

115

SECTION 66. This section *authorizes the Secretary of State to terminate the order restricting discharge* if he is satisfied that it is no longer required for the protection of the public. It also authorizes him, during the period of an order restricting discharge, to discharge the patient either absolutely or subject to conditions and, in the latter case, to recall him to hospital at any time while the order restricting discharge is still in force.

Under this section, the *Secretary of State is required to refer to a Mental Health Review Tribunal for their advice* within two months of receiving a written request to do so from a patient subject to an order restricting his discharge, which has been in force for a year or more. The patient may subsequently request this once during each period during which he could have applied to a Mental Health Review Tribunal had the order restricting his discharge not been in force. However, a patient recalled to hospital after being conditionally discharged may, in addition, make a request to the Secretary of State six months after the date of his recall to hospital.

SECTION 67. This section *authorizes a Magistrates' Court*, on conviction of a person over the age of 14 years of an offence punishable on summary conviction with imprisonment, *to commit him in custody to Quarter Sessions to be dealt with if it appears to the Court that an order restricting discharge should be made.* The Court of Quarter Sessions may make a hospital order with or without an order restricting discharge or may deal with the offender in any other manner the Magistrates' Court might have dealt with him. (*See* note on section 60.)

SECTION 68. This section *authorizes the Magistrates' Court to order the patient's admission to hospital* (with the hospital's consent) *instead of committing him in custody, pending his appearance at Quarter Sessions.* Such an order has the same effect as if the patient had been admitted to hospital subject to an order restricting his discharge. (*See* note on section 60.)

SECTION 69. This section *authorizes a patient*, subject to an order restricting his discharge made by a Court of Quarter Sessions or under section 67, *to appeal against the order to the Court of Criminal Appeal*, who may deal with the appeal as though it were also an appeal against the hospital order itself.

(This section was repealed by the Criminal Justice Act, 1967.)

SECTION 70. This section *authorizes a patient* subject to a hospital order or guardianship order made by a Magistrates' Court without convicting him *to appeal against the order to Quarter Sessions*; it also *authorizes a child or young person* brought before a Juvenile Court as in need of care or protection or as beyond the control of his parent or guardian *to appeal to Quarter Sessions* against such hospital or

116

guardianship order as the Court may make. His parent or guardian may similarly appeal.

The right of appeal of a child or a young person is now conferred by section 2 (12) of the Children and Young Persons Act, 1969. (*See* note on section 60.)

SECTION 72. This section *authorizes the Secretary of State to direct the transfer of a person serving a sentence of imprisonment to a hospital* (*not* a mental nursing home) *if* he is satisfied on the reports of *at least two* medical practitioners that the person is suffering from mental illness, psychopathic disorder, subnormality or severe subnormality which warrants the detention of the patient in hospital for medical treatment, and that this is in the public interest. *At least one* of the medical practitioners giving reports must be approved by the local health authority as having special experience in the diagnosis or treatment of mental disorders. Each medical practitioner must describe the patient as suffering from the *same one* form of mental disorder, although either or both may describe him as suffering from other forms as well. A direction under this section is valid for a period of fourteen days beginning with the date on which it was given.

SECTION 73. This section *authorizes the Secretary of State, if* he is satisfied on similar reports to those required under section 72 that a person is suffering from mental illness or severe subnormality which warrants the detention of the patient in hospital for medical treatment, *to order that person's transfer to hospital* from the various types of custody specified in the section or from civil imprisonment or from detention in prison as an alien. Except where the patient falls within the last two categories the restrictions of section 65 apply to him (after his transfer to hospital) (section 74).

SECTION 75. This section *authorizes the Secretary of State to direct the transfer back to prison of any patient* subject to an order restricting his discharge, on notification by the responsible medical officer that he no longer requires treatment for mental disorder, *provided the period of his prison sentence has not expired.*

SECTION 76. This section similarly *authorizes the Secretary of State* to take this step under similar circumstances *in the case of patients transferred to hospital under section* 73. This section also *authorizes a Court to make a hospital order* (with or without an order restricting discharge) in the case of patients specified under section 73, *if* it appears impracticable or inappropriate to bring him before the Court, *provided* the Court is satisfied on the oral evidence of *at least two medical practitioners* (one approved by the local health authority) that the person is suffering from mental illness or severe subnormality which warrants his detention in hospital for medical treatment, and that it is proper to make such an order.

SECTION 79. This section *authorizes the Secretary of State to direct that a child or young person detained* in an approved school should *be placed under the guardianship of a local health authority* or of any such other person approved by a local health authority, *if* he is satisfied on the reports required under section 72 that the child or young person is suffering from mental illness, psychopathic disorder, subnormality or severe subnormality which warrants the reception of the patient into guardianship under this Act, and that this is in the public interest.

As a result of the Children and Young Persons Act, 1969, *the Secretary of State no longer has powers to make guardianship orders under this section.* However, he has power under section 27 (3) of the 1969 Act to require a local authority to comply with his directions in relation to a particular child *provided that,* in his opinion, the protection of members of the public makes it necessary. Approved schools are now known as community homes.

## PART VI

### *REMOVAL AND RETURN OF PATIENTS WITHIN UNITED KINGDOM ETC.*

These matters are dealt with in sections 81–96, subject to a number of consequential amendments resulting from the later Mental Health (Scotland) Act, 1960, and the Mental Health Act (Northern Ireland) 1961.

## PART VII

### *SPECIAL HOSPITALS*

SECTION 97. This section *authorizes the Minister of Health to provide special hospitals* under his control and management (section 98) for persons subject to detention who, in the opinion of the Minister, require treatment under conditions of special security on account of their dangerous, violent or criminal propensities.

SECTION 99. This section *authorizes the Minister to direct the transfer of any patient from a special hospital to any other type of hospital.*

## PART VIII

### *MANAGEMENT OF PROPERTY AND AFFAIRS OF PATIENTS*

This is dealt with in sections 100–121, which are principally concerned with the appointment by the Lord Chancellor of '*nominated judges*', the *Master* and *Deputy Master of the Court of Protection* and *Medical* and *Legal Lord Chancellor's Visitors*, and the appointment by any of the foregoing of a receiver, and with the functions and powers of each in the management of the property and affairs of patients while they are mentally disordered.

There have been minor consequential amendments of this part of the Act as a result of the Administration of Justice Act, 1969, and the Courts Act, 1971.

# PART IX
*MISCELLANEOUS AND GENERAL*
## Powers and Proceedings of Mental Health Review Tribunals

SECTION 122. This section *requires all applications to Mental Health Review Tribunals to be made in writing* to the appropriate Tribunal for the area in which the hospital or nursing home in which the patient is detained is situated or in which the patient is residing under guardianship.

SECTION 123. This section *authorizes a Mental Health Review Tribunal to order a patient's discharge from detention if* they are satisfied that the patient is not suffering from mental illness, psychopathic disorder, subnormality or severe subnormality and that it is not necessary, in the interests of his health or safety or for the protection of others, for him to be detained and that he is not likely to act in a manner dangerous to other persons or himself. Similarly a *Mental Health Review Tribunal may direct a patient's discharge from guardianship if* they are satisfied it is not necessary in his interests or for the protection of others for him to remain under guardianship.

If they do not order discharge, a Mental Health Review Tribunal may direct that the form of mental disorder specified in the application order or direction be amended to a more appropriate form if they are satisfied that the patient is suffering from this.

## Ill-treatment of Patients

SECTION 126. This section *renders it an offence* for any officer on the staff of a hospital or mental nursing home, for anyone otherwise employed there or for any of the managers *to ill-treat or wilfully neglect a patient receiving treatment* for mental disorder *as an in-patient*, or on the premises of the hospital or home while the patient is attending there for treatment for mental disorder *as an out-patient*. It is also an offence for any individual to ill-treat or wilfully neglect a mentally disordered person while he is subject to his *guardianship* under the Act or in his custody or care.

The *penalties* for the above offences are, *on summary conviction*, a term of imprisonment not exceeding six months, or a fine not

119

exceeding £100, or both, or, *on conviction on indictment*, a term of imprisonment not exceeding two years, or a fine, or both.

## Amendment of Sexual Offences Act, 1956

SECTION 127. This section *amends the Sexual Offences Act*, 1956, in that it makes it an offence for a man to have unlawful sexual intercourse with a woman suffering from *severe* subnormality (but not with a *subnormal* woman, except under section 128) *provided* he knows or has reason to suspect her to be severely subnormal.

## Sexual Intercourse with Patients

SECTION 128. This section *renders it an offence* for an officer on the staff of a hospital or mental nursing home, for anyone otherwise employed there or for any of the managers *to have unlawful sexual intercourse on hospital premises* with a woman receiving treatment for mental disorder there either *as an in-patient* or *as an out-patient*.

It is also an offence for a man to have unlawful sexual intercourse with a mentally disordered woman subject to his *guardianship* or otherwise in his custody or care under this Act or as a resident in a residential home for mentally disordered persons.

*In each case under this section it must be shown that the man knew or had reason to suspect that the woman was a mentally disordered person.*

*No action may be taken under this section without the consent of the Director of Public Prosecutions.*

The *penalty* for this offence *on conviction or indictment* is a term of imprisonment not exceeding two years.

## Assisting Patients to Absent Themselves without Leave

SECTION 129. This section *renders it an offence to induce or knowingly assist a patient detained in hospital or subject to guardianship under this Act to absent himself without leave* or to escape from legal custody, or knowingly to harbour a patient absent without leave, or to assist him to prevent, hinder or interfere with his being taken into custody or returned to hospital or where he should be under guardianship.

The *penalties* for the above offences are, *on summary conviction*, a term of imprisonment not exceeding six months or a fine not exceeding £100, or both, or, *on conviction on indictment*, a term of imprisonment not exceeding two years, or a fine, or both.

120

## Authority to Search for and Remove Patients

SECTION 135. This section *authorizes a Justice of the Peace to issue a warrant authorizing a constable to enter,* if need be by force, any premises within his jurisprudence specified in the warrant, and, if thought fit, *to remove from there to a place of safety,* pending arrangements for his treatment or care, any person (who need not be named in the warrant) whom the magistrate has, on information sworn by a mental welfare officer, reasonable cause to suspect to be suffering from mental disorder and to have been or to be ill-treated, neglected or not kept under proper control or to be living alone and unable to care for himself. *The constable must be accompanied* in the execution of the warrant by a *mental welfare officer* and by a *medical practitioner.*

This section also *authorizes a Justice of the Peace,* on the sworn evidence of any constable or any other person authorized under this Act to take a patient to any place or to take into custody or retake a patient, *to issue a warrant authorizing any named constable to enter any premises,* if need be by force, and *to remove from there any patient liable to be taken or retaken, provided* admission to the premises has been refused or if such a refusal is apprehended. The constable *may* be accompanied in the execution of the warrant by a *medical practitioner* or by *any person authorized* under the Act to take or retake the patient.

A patient removed to a *place of safety* under this section may be detained there for a period not exceeding seventy-two hours.

A *'place of safety'* is defined as residential accommodation provided by a local authority under Part III of the National Health Service Act, 1946, or under Part III of the National Assistance Act, 1948, a hospital as defined in this Act, a police station, a mental nursing home or residential home for mentally disordered persons, or any other suitable place, the occupier of which is willing temporarily to receive the patient.

## Mentally Disordered Persons found in Public Places

SECTION 136. This section *authorizes a constable to remove to a place of safety an apparently mentally disordered person* in immediate need of care or control, found by him in a place to which the public have access, *provided* he considers it necessary in the interests of that person or for the protection of other persons.

A person removed in this way may be detained in the *place of safety* for a period *not exceeding seventy-two hours* so that he may be examined by a medical practitioner and interviewed by a mental welfare officer and any necessary arrangements made for his treatment or care.

121

## Criminal Responsibility

*The fact that a person is suffering from one of the forms of mental disorder described in the Mental Health Act, 1959, whether or not he is subject to a hospital detention order or guardianship, is not of itself a defence to a criminal or civil charge.* However, under the circumstances described in section 60, a Magistrates' Court may, in the case of a person suffering from mental illness or severe subnormality, order his detention in hospital or reception into guardianship under the Act, *without convicting him.* In other cases a mentally disordered person may be found *unfit to plead* because he is incapable of understanding the charge against him, or instructing his counsel, and in this case he is not put on trial but ordered to be detained until Her Majesty's pleasure be known.

If a mentally disordered person is fit to plead to a criminal charge he may be found *legally insane if* it can be shown that his mental disorder was at the time he committed the offence such that he did not know what he was doing, or if he did, that he did not know that what he was doing was wrong (the so-called McNaughton rules). Upon finding a person legally insane the Court orders him to be detained until Her Majesty's pleasure be known.

## Contracts

*A contract entered into by a subnormal or severely subnormal person is binding upon him and upon the person contracting with him, unless* it can be shown that the former person was incapable of understanding the terms of the contract and the other person knew that his mental state was such that he did not understand what he was doing. If both these conditions are fulfilled, the contract entered into becomes voidable at the option of the subnormal or severely subnormal person or of his committee or trustees.

## Testamentary Capacity

Legally, *the ability of the subnormal or severely subnormal person to execute a valid will is governed by the same conditions as in the case of the mentally ill.* Briefly, a will is valid only if the testator is able, at the time he makes it, to recall and keep clearly in his mind the nature and extent of his property and the persons who have claims on his bounty, his judgement and will being so unclouded as to enable him to determine the relative strength of these claims.

## Marriage

*There is no law to prevent the mentally subnormal from marrying, but* a marriage is voidable under the Matrimonial Causes Act, 1950, if at the time of the marriage either of the parties was suffering from mental disorder within the meaning of the Mental Health Act, 1959, of such a kind or to such an extent as to be unfitted for marriage and the procreation of children, or was subject to recurrent attacks of insanity or epilepsy, *provided* that the petitioner was at the time of the marriage ignorant of the facts alleged, that the proceedings were instituted *within a year* from the date of the marriage and that marital intercourse, with the consent of the petitioner, has not taken place since the discovery by the petitioner of the existence of the grounds for a decree. Mental disorder, of course, includes subnormality or severe subnormality.

## Representation of the People Act, 1949

*The fact that a subnormal or severely subnormal person is detained in hospital under an order does not, of itself, prohibit him from voting provided his name appears on the Register of Voters for the constituency which includes his place of residence immediately before his admission to the hospital.*

# THE MENTAL HEALTH (SCOTLAND) ACT, 1960

The provisions of the Mental Health (Scotland) Act, 1960, differ from those of the Mental Health Act, 1959, in the following main respects:

The numbering of sections dealing with similar provisions does not necessarily correspond in the two Acts.

## PART I

SECTION 1 repeals the Lunacy (Scotland) Acts, 1857 to 1913, and the Mental Deficiency (Scotland) Acts, 1913 and 1940.

SECTION 2 establishes in place of the *General Board of Control for Scotland*, whose dissolution is effected by section 3, the Mental Welfare Commission for Scotland:

## *THE MENTAL WELFARE COMMISSION FOR SCOTLAND*

The Act requires that the Mental Welfare Commission shall consist of *no fewer than seven and not more than nine commissioners*, including its *Chairman*. It specifies that at least one commissioner shall be a *woman*, at least three shall be *medical practitioners* and that one shall have been, for a period of at least five years, either a *Member of the Faculty of Advocates* or a *solicitor*.

The Commissioners are appointed by Her Majesty on the recommendation of the Secretary of State, and *members of the Civil Service are specifically barred* from membership of the Commission.

A *quorum* of the Mental Welfare Commission is defined as *four* Commissioners, including at least one medical commissioner.

SECTION 4. This section *defines the functions and duties of the Mental Welfare Commission*, which include many of those formerly undertaken by the General Board of Control. Thus, the Mental Welfare Commission has the general function of protecting the persons and interests of those whose mental disorder prevents their doing so adequately themselves. For this purpose the Commission has *authority to discharge* such patients from detention in hospital or guardianship, and a duty to inquire into any case where there may be ill-treatment, deficiency in care or treatment, or improper detention of a mentally disordered person, or a risk of loss or damage to his property. The Commission, represented by at least one medical member, is *required to visit regularly and to grant private interviews on request* to patients detained in hospital or subject to guardianship, and to draw the attention of the hospital board of management or local authority to any apparent shortcomings of the type specified above concerning any patient under their care.

Authority is imposed on the Commission to advise the Secretary of State on any matter arising out of the Act which he may refer to it and to draw his attention to any matter under the Act of which it feels he should be aware.

## TYPES OF MENTAL DISORDER

SECTION 6. This section *defines 'mental disorder'* as 'mental illness or mental deficiency however caused or manifested'. That is to say, the Mental Health (Scotland) Act, 1960, recognizes only two types of mental disorder and *retains the term 'mental deficiency' without defining it*.

## PART II
### LOCAL AUTHORITY SERVICES
**Functions of Local Health Authority**

SECTION 7. This section *authorizes the provision by local health authorities* of the same services for the mentally disordered as does section 6 of the Mental Health Act, 1959, with the *exception* of specific mention of occupation and training facilities and with the *addition* of the *ascertainment of mental defectives* not of school age and the *supervision of mental defectives not subject to guardianship or detention in a hospital*. The description *'mental health officer'* replaces 'mental welfare officer'.

N.B. Local *health* authorities' responsibilities under this section were transferred to the corresponding local authorities by the Social Work (Scotland) Act, 1968, and not specifically to their social service departments as in the English Health Services and Public Health Act, 1968.

SECTION 12. This section *imposes a duty on local health authorities to provide*, or secure the provision of, suitable training and occupation, not only for children under the age of 16 years unsuitable for education or training in a special school, but also for mental defectives over that age, and to arrange the necessary transport.

(N.B. The local health authorities' responsibilities under this section for children under 16 were transferred to the local authorities' education departments, and for older mental defectives to their social services departments, by the Social Work (Scotland) Act, 1968.)

**Local Health Authority's Powers to compel Attendance at Training Centres**

SECTION 13. This section corresponds, in effect, to section 12, Mental Health Act, 1959, with the exception that it is the Secretary of State who is required to reach a decision if the parent is aggrieved. (*See* note on section 7.)

## PART III

### PRIVATE HOSPITALS AND RESIDENTIAL HOMES

SECTIONS 15–18. These sections differ from sections 14–17 in the Mental Health Act, 1959, in that the premises are designated as '*private hospitals*' and not as 'mental nursing homes', and in that the functions of registration, imposition of conditions and inspection are vested in the Secretary of State and not the local health authority.

## PART IV

### HOSPITAL CARE AND GUARDIANSHIP

It is in these sections that the Mental Health (Scotland) Act, 1960, differs most significantly from the Mental Health Act, 1959.

SECTION 23. This section, in effect, *excludes from compulsory admission to hospital* (except under the provisions for emergency admission) or *from reception into guardianship, patients over the age of* 21 *years*, who would satisfy the definitions of *subnormality* and *psychopathic disorder* in the Mental Health Act, 1959. It imposes limitations (with exceptions) on the compulsory detention in hospital or under guardianship, past the age of 25 years, of such patients, similar to the limitations in the latter Act.

### Informal Admission of Patients to Hospital

Section 23 also *permits* the informal admission of mentally disordered patients *without* the mention of parental rights below the age of 16 years implied in section 5, Mental Health Act, 1959.

### COMPULSORY ADMISSION TO HOSPITAL AND RECEPTION INTO GUARDIANSHIP

*Legal authority* for detention in hospital or reception into guardianship is retained in the Mental Health (Scotland) Act, 1960, in the person of the *Sheriff*, who has to *approve all applications before they become effective*.

There is no separate provision in the Mental Health (Scotland) Act, 1960, for admission for *twenty-eight days' observation*, this, in effect, being incorporated in the procedure for the admission of patients to hospital for treatment.

126

**Admission for Treatment**

SECTION 24. The *application for admission*, founded on *two medical recommendations*, has to be made by the *nearest* relative (defined in section 45) or by the mental health officer, who can act *in spite* of the nearest relative's objections (section 26) although he must inform him of his *right of appeal* to the Sheriff (section 28).

SECTION 27. For the purposes of making their recommendations the medical practitioners may examine the patient together *only* when no objection has been made by the patient or his nearest relative.

*One of the medical practitioners has to be approved for the purposes of this section by the Regional Hospital Board*, and not by the local health authority, as in the Mental Health Act, 1959.

*Not more than one* of the medical recommendations may be given by a medical officer in the service of a local authority, and neither by a medical practitioner who is making the application. The other exclusions listed in section 28, Mental Health Act, 1959, do not apply, although the relationship of either medical practitioner to the patient, or any pecuniary interest he may have in the admission of the patient into hospital, has to be stated in his recommendation. Medical practitioners on the staff of a *private* hospital or other private accommodation to which the patient is to be admitted are specifically excluded from giving either medical recommendation.

SECTION 28. The *application for admission* has to be submitted to the Sheriff for his approval *within seven days* of the last date on which the patient was examined for the purposes of any medical recommendation accompanying the application. The Sheriff, in considering the application, may make such enquiries and see such persons (including the patient) as he thinks fit. Where the patient's relative has objected to the application, he must afford that relative, and any witness the latter may call, an opportunity of being heard. At the patient's or applicant's request or the Sheriff's wish, these proceedings shall be conducted in private.

SECTION 29. The *patient may be admitted* to the hospital named in the application at any time *within a period of seven days* from the date on which the Sheriff approved the application.

The board of management of the hospital are required to send to the Mental Welfare Commission, *within seven days* of the patient's admission, copies of the application and medical recommendations.

The *responsible medical officer* is required to examine the patient himself, or to obtain from another medical practitioner a report on the condition of the patient, *within the period of seven days ending on the twenty-eighth day after his admission*. If the responsible medical officer does not then discharge the patient, he must inform the Mental Welfare Commission, the nearest relative and the board of management (cf. section 25, Mental Health Act, 1959).

127

## ADMISSION IN CASE OF EMERGENCY

SECTION 31. This section *authorizes a medical practitioner*, who has personally examined a mentally disordered person, to make a medical recommendation concerning him *on the same day*, which permits the patient's removal to hospital *within three days* and his detention there *for a period not exceeding seven days, provided* the medical practitioner considers the necessity for this is so urgent that compliance with the provisions of section 24 would involve unreasonable delay.

The medical practitioner is required, when practicable, to seek the consent of a relative or mental health officer to the making of an emergency recommendation, which must be accompanied by a statement that he has done so or of the reason for his failure to obtain that consent.

The board of management of the hospital to which the patient is admitted must, without delay, where practicable, inform the nearest relative and some responsible person residing with the patient of the latter's emergency admission.

## APPLICATIONS IN RESPECT OF PATIENTS ALREADY IN HOSPITAL

SECTION 32. This section *authorizes the use of the application for admission and emergency recommendation procedures for patients already in hospital*, and the latter procedure may therefore be used in an emergency to detain *informal* admissions pending action under section 24.

## GUARDIANSHIP

SECTION 25. This section *authorizes*, subject to approval by the Sheriff of the application, the *reception into guardianship* of either a local health authority or of any other person (including the applicant himself) approved by that authority of any person suffering from mental illness or mental deficiency which requires or is susceptible to medical treatment and warrants his reception into guardianship *provided* that this is in the interests of the patient or for the protection of other persons.

The same categories of patients are excluded by section 23 from liability to reception into guardianship as from liability to detention in hospital, and the same general provisions as to applications, reports to the Mental Welfare Commission and nearest relative and medical recommendations apply to guardianship cases as to hospital cases.

The effect of a guardianship application, approved by the Sheriff and forwarded to the local health authority within seven days, is

128

to confer on the authority or person named, to the exclusion of any other person, the same powers over the patient as would be the case if they or he were the father of the patient and the patient were a *pupil child.* However, the guardian is given no power with respect to any property of the patient and is prohibited from administering corporal punishment to him (section 29). (*See* note on section 7.)

## LEAVE OF ABSENCE FROM HOSPITAL

SECTION 35. There is *no automatic discharge* from hospital detention *after six month's authorized leave of absence* as in the Mental Health Act, 1959, but the responsible medical officer is required *within fourteen days* to inform the Mental Welfare Commission of the patient's name and address on any leave *exceeding twenty-eight days,* including extensions of this duration of a previous six months' leave period. The responsible medical officer is also required to notify the commission *within fourteen days of the patient's return.*

## ABSENCE WITHOUT LEAVE

SECTION 36. The provisions of this section are similar to those of the Mental Health Act, 1959, with the important variation in the period during which patients absent without leave, who are liable to detention in hospital or subject to guardianship, may be taken into custody, i.e. in the case of a *mental defective—within three months,* in the case of a *patient subject to an emergency recommendation— within seven days* and in *any other case—twenty-eight days,* beginning in each case with the first day of their absence.

## TRANSFER OF PATIENTS

SECTION 37. A *patient may be transferred* from one hospital to another with the consent of the board of management of the two hospitals or, from hospital to the guardianship of a local health authority or someone approved by the authority, with the consent of the board of management and the proposed guardian. A patient subject to guardianship may be transferred by a local health authority to the guardianship of another person with the latter's consent, but the Mental Welfare Commission's consent and that of the hospital board of management are required before a local authority can transfer a patient from guardianship to hospital and, in *all cases,* either the consent of the guardian must be obtained or, if this is refused, the approval of the Sheriff to the transfer must be sought. The board of management of the hospital to which the patient is transferred or the local health authority concerned, as the case may be, are required to notify the nearest relative and the Mental Welfare Commission *within seven days* of the date of transfer. (*See* note on section 7.)

## DURATION OF AUTHORITY FOR DETENTION OR GUARDIANSHIP AND DISCHARGE OF PATIENTS

SECTION 39. The *initial duration and period of renewal* specified in this section are similar to those in section 43, Mental Health Act, 1959, but in this case the responsible medical officer is required to obtain, *two months prior to the expiry of authority* for detention or guardianship, a report from *another* medical practitioner on the patient's condition, and to consider this report in assessing the need for continued detention or guardianship, having regard to their necessity in the interests of the health or safety of the patient and for the protection of other persons.

In each case where the responsible medical officer considers continued detention or guardianship necessary he is required to furnish a report to that effect, in the prescribed form, with the report of the second medical practitioner, to the board of management of the hospital or local health authority, as the case may be, and also to the Mental Welfare Commission.

The board of management or local health authority are required to notify the patient and his nearest relative or guardian when authority for detention or guardianship is renewed. (*See* note on section 7.)

*On attaining the age of* 16 *years* a patient may *appeal to the Sheriff* to order his discharge, within the period for which the authority for his detention or guardianship is renewed.

SECTION 40. This section *requires the responsible medical officer, board of management or local health authority* to take action similar to that specified in section 39, *within two months of the twenty-fifth birthday* of a mental defective who has been continuously detained in hospital or subject to guardianship since attaining the age of 21 years, or of a patient detained in hospital or subject to guardianship who is suffering from mental illness which manifests itself only as persistent abnormally aggressive or seriously irresponsible conduct. (*See* note on section 7.)

Where the authority for detention or guardianship is continued the patient and his nearest relative have, *within a period of twenty-eight days*, beginning with the patient's twenty-fifth birthday, the right of appeal to the Sheriff for the patient's discharge.

## DISCHARGE OF PATIENTS

SECTION 43. This section *authorizes the following persons to make an order discharging a patient from detention or guardianship:*

130

The *responsible medical officer* or the *Mental Welfare Commission*, in the case of a patient detained in hospital or subject to guardianship (but not the responsible medical officer without the consent of the board of management when the patient is detained in a *State hospital*).

The *Sheriff*, when an appeal has been made to him under sections 39, 40 or 44 of this Act.

The *nearest relative*, or the *board of management*, in the case of a detained patient, and the *local health authority*, in the case of a patient subject to guardianship, with the consent in *both* cases of the responsible medical officer who, when he does not consent, is required to furnish a report that, in his opinion, the patient cannot be discharged without being a danger to himself or to others. In the absence of such a report the *discharge order takes effect at the end of a period of seven days after it is made.* (*See* note on section 7.)

## RESTRICTIONS ON DISCHARGE BY NEAREST RELATIVE

SECTION 44. This section *requires the nearest relative to give not less than seven days' notice in writing* to the board of management or local health authority of *an order to discharge a patient* liable to detention in hospital or subject to guardianship, and *authorizes the continued detention of the patient, against the nearest relative's wishes,* if the responsible medical officer reports to the appropriate authority, *within the period of notice,* that in his opinion the patient's mental disorder is such as would warrant his admission to hospital or reception into guardianship, or if the patient is already detained in hospital, that he would be likely to act in a manner dangerous to others or to himself if discharged. It also *denies the relative the right to order discharge again during a period of six months* beginning with the date of the responsible medical officer's report, but requires the relative to be informed of the report and confers on the relative the *right to appeal to the Sheriff within the period of twenty-eight days,* beginning with the day on which he was informed.

This section also *precludes the nearest relative from making a discharge order in respect of a patient detained in a State hospital.* (*See* note on section 7.)

## PART V
## DETENTION OF PATIENTS CONCERNED IN CRIMINAL PROCEEDINGS AND TRANSFER OF PATIENTS UNDER SENTENCE

SECTION 54. This section *authorizes a court,* when they are satisfied on the written or oral evidence of a medical practitioner that a person charged with an offence, whom they are remanding or

131

committing for trial, is suffering from mental disorder, *to commit him to hospital* instead of remanding him in custody, *provided* the court is also satisfied that that hospital is available for his admission and suitable for his detention.

A person committed to hospital in this way is liable to be detained there for the period for which he is remanded or for the period of committal *unless*, before the expiration of that period, he is liberated in due course of law, or the responsible medical officer reports to the court that the person committed is not suffering from mental disorder of a nature or degree which warrants his admission to hospital under part IV of the Act. In the latter case the court may commit him to any prison or other institution to which he might have been committed had he not been committed to hospital, or may otherwise deal with him according to law.

SECTION 55. This section *authorizes the High Court of Judiciary or the Sheriff Court* (in the case of a person convicted of an offence other than an offence the sentence for which is fixed by law), or a Sheriff Court (in the case of a person remitted to that court by a court of summary jurisdiction other than a Sheriff Court, before which he has been charged with any act or omission constituting an offence punishable with imprisonment), *to order that person's admission to and detention in a specified hospital or to place him under the guardianship of a local health authority provided* that the court is satisfied, on the written or oral evidence of two medical practitioners, that the offender is suffering from mental disorder of a nature or degree which, in the case of a person *under* 21 *years of age*, would warrant his admission to a hospital or his reception into guardianship under part IV of this Act and that, having regard to all the circumstances, this is the most suitable method of dealing with the case. The court must also be satisfied that the hospital specified will be able to admit the patient *within a period of twenty-eight days* beginning with the date of the making of the order, or that the local health authority or other person specified is willing to receive the offender into guardianship. (*See* note on section 7.)

A *Sheriff Court* may make an order under this section of the Act without convicting a person charged summarily before it *provided* the court is satisfied he did the act.

A *State hospital may not be specified* in a hospital order *unless* the court is satisfied, on the evidence of the medical practitioners, that the offender, on account of his dangerous, violent or criminal propensities, requires treatment under conditions of special security and cannot suitably be cared for in a hospital other than a State hospital.

A *duty is imposed on the prosecutor* to bring before the court evidence of the mental condition of any person charged who appears to him to be suffering from mental disorder.

132

SECTION 56. This section *authorizes a Sheriff Court* (in the case of a child or young person brought before that court—or before a Juvenile Court and remitted to the Sheriff Court—under section 66 or section 68 of the Children and Young Persons (Scotland) Act, 1937) *to make a hospital or guardianship order provided* the court is satisfied that the child or young person is in need of care and protection, or that his parent or guardian is unable to control him, and that the conditions which are required under section 55 for the making of a hospital order or guardianship order are, so far as applicable, satisfied in the case of the child or young person.

The court must also be satisfied that the *parent or guardian understands* the results which will follow from the order and *consents* to its being made.

*A duty is imposed on the person bringing the child or young person before the court* to bring such evidence as may be available of the mental condition of the child if he appears to that person to be suffering from mental disorder.

N.B. Juvenile Courts have now been abolished in Scotland and the following procedure substituted by Part III of the Social Work (Scotland) Act, 1968: An official with the title of 'Reporter' considers whether any child referred to him as having committed an offence is in need of compulsory measures of care and, if so, arranges for him to be brought with his parents before a 'Children's Hearing', which is a sitting of a treatment authority for each local authority area. The Children's Hearing has no power to adjudicate on whether or not the child committed the alleged offence and where the facts alleged are disputed, the hearing cannot proceed with the case unless it is referred to the Sheriff and he finds the facts established. The Children's Hearing then has the power to impose (by means of a 'supervision requirement') what compulsory measures of care it considers are required. For the purposes of the Act, 'child' means basically a person under 16 years of age but includes a person aged 16 and over but under 18 if he has a supervision requirement in force in respect of him.)

SECTION 58. This section *cancels the power of the nearest relative to order discharge* of a patient admitted to hospital as a result of a court order and *removes the age limits to the detention in hospital or under guardianship of patients* whose only manifestation of mental illness is persistent abnormally aggressive or irresponsible conduct, or whose mental deficiency is not such that they are incapable of living an independent life or of guarding themselves against serious exploitation.

SECTION 59. This section *authorizes the patient's detention in a place of safety pending his admission to hospital within a period of twenty-eight days*, beginning with the day on which the hospital order was made by the court.

SECTION 60. This section *authorizes a court making a hospital order to impose an order restricting the patient's discharge and any of the following special restrictions,* either indefinitely or for a specified period, where this is considered necessary for the protection of the public *provided* that the evidence of the medical practitioner approved by the Regional Hospital Board was given *orally* in Court.

During the period that discharge is restricted the normal limit to the duration of the authority for detention does not apply and a guardianship order may not be made in respect of the patient.

The *consent of the Secretary of State* is necessary before the patient can be transferred to another hospital or before he can be granted leave, and he can be recalled from leave at any time while the order restricting discharge is in force. The Secretary of State's consent is also necessary before the patient may be discharged by any of the persons who normally have this power.

SECTION 61. This section *authorizes the Secretary of State to terminate the order restricting discharge if* he is satisfied that it is no longer required for the protection of the public. It also authorizes him, during the period of an order restricting discharge, to discharge the patient either absolutely or subject to conditions and, in the latter case, to recall him to hospital at any time while the order restricting discharge is still in force.

SECTION 62. This section *gives a patient a right of appeal against a hospital or guardianship order or order restricting discharge made by a Court.*

SECTION 65. This section *authorizes the Secretary of State to apply to the Sheriff to direct the transfer of a person in custody, awaiting trial or sentence, to a hospital (not* a private hospital), when it appears to the Secretary of State that the person is suffering from mental disorder of a nature or degree which warrants his admission to a hospital under part IV of the Act. If the Sheriff is satisfied of this, on the reports of *two* medical practitioners, he may make a hospital order, which is *subject to a restriction on discharge of unlimited duration. At least one* of the medical practitioners giving reports must be approved by the Regional Hospital Board as having special experience in the diagnosis or treatment of mental disorders. Each medical practitioner must describe the patient as suffering from the *same one* form of mental disorder, although either, or both, may describe him as suffering from other forms as well. A detention order under this section is *valid for a period of fourteen days* beginning with the date on which it is given.

The patient remains liable to be detained in hospital, *but not subject to a restriction order*, if the proceedings against him are dropped, or after his case has been disposed of by the Court to which he was committed or by which he was remanded, unless the Court pass a sentence of imprisonment or make a guardianship order concerning him, or the responsible medical officer notifies the Secretary of State that he no longer requires treatment for mental disorder (section 68).

SECTION 66. This section *authorizes the Secretary of State*, if he is satisfied on similar reports to those required under section 65 that a person is suffering from mental disorder which warrants his admission to hospital, *to direct that person's transfer to hospital from prison* in which he is serving a sentence as a civil prisoner or detained as an alien. This direction is *valid for a period of fourteen days* beginning with the date on which it is given.

*A person dealt with in this way may appeal to the Sheriff within three months*, and if his transfer order is cancelled the Secretary of State is required to direct his return to prison.

SECTION 67. This section *authorizes the Secretary of State to impose restriction on discharge of prisoners transferred to hospital.*

SECTION 69. This section *authorizes the Secretary of State to direct the transfer back to prison* of any patient subject to a direction restricting his discharge, on notification by the responsible medical officer that he no longer requires treatment for mental disorder, *provided the period of his prison sentence has not expired.*

The responsible medical officer is required to assess the need for the continued detention of a patient *after a direction restricting his discharge has ceased to have effect*, on the basis of a report on his condition obtained by the responsible medical officer from *another* medical practitioner *within a period of twenty-eight days of the expiry of that order*. If the responsible medical officer considers that the patient's continued detention in hospital is necessary in the interests of the health or safety of the patient or for the protection of other persons, he is required to furnish a report to this effect, in the prescribed form, with the other medical practitioner's report, to the hospital board of management and Mental Welfare Commission. The patient is then treated as though he had been admitted to hospital on a hospital order *without restriction on his discharge* on the date the previous restriction direction expired, and the patient and his nearest relative must be informed of this by the board of management.

SECTION 71. This section *authorizes the Secretary of State to direct that a child or young person detained in an approved school be placed under the guardianship of a local health authority*, if he is satisfied on the reports required under section 65 that the child or young person is suffering from mental disorder of a nature or degree which warrants his reception into guardianship under this Act and that this is in the public interest. (*See* note on section 7.)

## PART VI
### *REMOVAL AND RETURN OF PATIENTS WITHIN THE UNITED KINGDOM, ETC.*

SECTIONS 73–88. These sections, with the amendments they contain to the Mental Health Act, 1959, *authorize the Secretary of State/ Minister of Health to direct the transfer of a patient liable to be detained or subject to guardianship in Scotland, England, Wales or Northern Ireland to any other of these countries if* he considers this to be in the patient's interest.

The sections similarly *authorize the taking into custody* anywhere within Scotland, England, Wales or Northern Ireland of any patient absent without leave.

## PART VII
### *STATE HOSPITALS*

The *State hospitals* in Scotland correspond to the *special hospitals* in England.

SECTION 89. This section *requires the Secretary of State to provide State hospitals* for mentally disordered patients subject to detention who require treatment under conditions of special security on account of their dangerous, violent or criminal propensities.

The Secretary of State is authorized to appoint committees to manage the State hospitals.

### *MISCELLANEOUS AND GENERAL*
#### Patient's Correspondence

SECTION 34. This section differs from section 36, Mental Health Act, 1959, only in the following list of persons which is substituted for that in the latter section:
1. The nearest relative of the patient.
2. The Secretary of State.
3. The Lord Advocate.
4. Any Member of the Commons House of Parliament.
5. Any Mental Welfare Commission or any Commissioner thereof.
6. Any Sheriff or Sheriff Clerk.
7. The Board of Management of the hospital.

## Ill-treatment of Patients

SECTION 95. As section 126, Mental Health Act, 1959, except that it specifies the amount of the maximum possible fine as £500 on conviction on indictment.

## Sexual Intercourse with Female Defectives

SECTION 96. This section *renders it an offence for a man to have unlawful sexual intercourse with a female defective,* for anyone to procure or encourage a female defective to have unlawful sexual intercourse, or for the owner or occupier of any premises or any person having or assisting in the management or control of the premises to induce a female defective to resort to or be on such premises for the purpose of unlawful sexual intercourse with any man, *provided* those persons had reason to know or had reason to suspect that the woman concerned was a defective incapable of living an independent life or of guarding herself against serious exploitation. The penalty for the above offence is, on conviction on indictment, a term of imprisonment not exceeding two years.

SECTION 97. This section, which *concerns sexual intercourse with patients,* is in all essential respects identical with section 128, Mental Health Act, 1959, except that the institution of proceedings is not dependent on the consent of the Director of Public Prosecutions.

## Assisting Patients to Absent Themselves without Leave

SECTION 98. As section 129, Mental Health Act, 1959, except that it specifies the amount of the maximum possible fine as £500 on conviction on indictment.

## Authority to Search For and Remove Patients

SECTION 103. This section *authorizes a mental health officer or medical commissioner,* on production of documentary proof of his authority, to demand admission at all reasonable times to inspect any place in which he has reasonable cause to believe that a person suffering from mental disorder is being ill-treated, neglected or not kept under proper control, or is living alone and unable to care for himself. When a Justice of the Peace, on sworn evidence in writing by either of these officers, is satisfied that he has been refused admission, or such refusal is apprehended, *the Justice may issue a warrant authorizing a constable to enter,* if need be by force, any premises specified in the warrant, and, if thought fit, *to remove any person suffering from mental disorder from there to a place of safety,* pending arrangements for his treatment or care. The constable *must* be accompanied in the execution of the warrant by a medical practitioner.

This section also authorizes a Justice of the Peace, on the sworn evidence in writing of any constable or any other person authorized under this Act (or under section 93, Mental Health Act, 1959) to take a patient to any place or to take into custody or retake a patient, *to issue a warrant authorizing any named constable to enter any premises*, if need be by force, and *to remove from there any patient liable to be taken or retaken provided* admission to the premises has been refused or if such a refusal is apprehended. The constable *may* be accompanied in the execution of the warrant by a *medical practitioner* or by *any person authorized* under the Act (or section 93, Mental Health Act, 1959) to take or retake the patient.

A patient removed to a *place of safety* under this section may be detained there for a period *not exceeding seventy-two hours*.

A *place of safety* means a hospital as defined by this Act, a residential home for persons suffering from mental disorder or any other suitable place, the occupier of which is willing temporarily to receive the patient, but shall *not* include a police station unless by reason of emergency there is no place as aforesaid available for receiving the patient.

### Mentally Disordered Persons found in Public Places

SECTION 104. As section 136, Mental Health Act, 1959, with the omission of the interview by a mental welfare officer, but with the *additional requirement* that the constable inform *without delay* some responsible person residing with the patient and the nearest relative of the patient.

# THE MENTAL HEALTH ACT (NORTHERN IRELAND), 1961

The Mental Health Act (Northern Ireland), 1961, recognizes three forms of mental disorder—*mental illness, arrested or incomplete development of mind* and *any other disorder or disability of mind*. Instead of the terms 'mentally subnormal' or 'mentally defective' used in the English and Scottish Acts it introduces the term '*person requiring special care*', who is defined as *someone suffering from arrested or incomplete development of mind* (whether arising from inherent causes or induced by disease or injury) *which renders him socially inefficient to such an extent that he requires supervision, training or control in his own interests or in the interests of other persons.* Two of the *criteria of social inefficiency* specified in the Act are, in fact, the definitions of the idiot and the imbecile in the Mental Deficiency Act, 1913, and the other two specified are *unsuitability for education at school* and the *need of care for the protection of others.*

The Mental Health Act (Northern Ireland), 1961, differs considerably from the Mental Health Act, 1959, and from the Mental Health (Scotland) Act, 1960, as regards the procedures for hospital detention and guardianship and the reader is referred to the Act itself for details.

## MENTAL HEALTH REVIEW TRIBUNAL

There is only one Mental Health Review Tribunal for Northern Ireland with membership and functions similar to those in England and Wales.

As a result of the reorganization of the health and social services which took place in Northern Ireland on 1 October, 1973, the *only fully integrated service for the mentally handicapped in the British Isles* was unfortunately destroyed by the abolition of the Northern Ireland Hospitals Authority, which had previously been responsible for both hospital and community care. Also abolished were its three special care management committees, whose duties included the ascertainment of persons requiring special care, their supervision, guardianship and training in the community and in residential accommodation, including hospitals. These duties are now the responsibility of four Area Boards for Health and Social Services, but at the time of writing it is not clear exactly how they are to be implemented.

# Index